PLANNING THE TOTAL LANDSCAPE: A GUIDE TO INTELLIGENT LAND USE

ABOUT THE BOOK AND AUTHOR

Planning the Total Landscape:
A Guide to Intelligent Land Use
Julius Gy. Fabos

Rapid changes in land use, especially in growing metropolitan areas, have created problems that increasingly indicate an urgent need for techniques and procedures for making intelligent land-use decisions. This book identifies the potential undesirable effects of land-use changes and provides techniques for estimating and minimizing them. Based on several years of research conducted by a team of thirty-four faculty and assistants, the study shows how planners and decision makers can benefit from such contemporary planning tools as remote sensing, statistical analysis, and computer technology, as well as a variety of evaluation procedures.

Part 1 describes the problems of contemporary urbanization and offers a set of planning principles and tools for working with the environmental landscape. These principles and tools are the basis of the procedures detailed in Part 2; the assessment procedures, in turn, are an essential part of the two current planning approaches—the holistic, landscape approach and the parametric approach—described in Part 3.

Julius Gy. Fabos, professor of landscape planning and director of the program in regional planning at the University of Massachusetts, received a masters degree in landscape architecture from Harvard University and a Ph.D. in resource planning and conservation from the University of Michigan. Dr. Fabos is also visiting professor at the Centre for Environmental Studies in Parkville, Australia.

PLANNING THE TOTAL LANDSCAPE: A GUIDE TO INTELLIGENT LAND USE

Julius Gy. Fabos

Routledge
Taylor & Francis Group
NEW YORK AND LONDON

First published in paperback 2024

First published 1979 by Westview Press, Inc.

Published 2019
by Routledge
605 Third Avenue, New York, NY 10158

and by Routledge
4 Park Square, Milton Park, Abingdon, Oxon OX14 4RN

Routledge is an imprint of the Taylor & Francis Group, an informa business

Library of Congress Cataloging in Publication Data
Fabos, Julius Gy.
Planning the total landscape.
Bibliography: p.
Includes index.
1. Land use—Planning. 2. Land use—Environmental aspects. 3. Metropolitan areas. 4. Land use—Planning—Massachusetts. I. Title.
HD111.F28 333.7'09744 78-3639

Publisher's Note
The publisher has gone to great lengths to ensure the quality of this reprint but points out that some imperfections in the original copies may be apparent.

ISBN 13: 978-0-367-28300-1 (hbk)
ISBN 13: 978-0-367-29846-3 (pbk)
ISBN 13: 978-0-429-30175-9 (ebk)

DOI: 10.4324/9780429301759

To Charles Eliot III, Benton MacKaye, and Ian McHarg,
whose writing and work were most inspirational to me.

CONTENTS

FIGURES AND TABLES

Figure

Table

ACKNOWLEDGMENTS

Environmental planning, by its very nature, draws on many influences and disciplines. This is true even when one takes a more limited aspect of environmental planning, such as urban decentralization from the point of view of landscape planning. The circumstances and individuals that influenced me are too numerous to mention.

The most significant influences on this book are three. First, I have been fortunate enough to take part in the landscape architecture program at the University of Massachusetts. During the past fourteen years, this program has grown under the direction of Ervin Zube, Paul Procopio, and Ross Whaley to include landscape planning and regional planning curricula. The departmental faculty and the program they developed were a constant stimulus to me. Second, our department has worked with several other departments at the university, and this exchange has provided me with many of the ideas included in this book. My work with ecologists, foresters, soil scientists, geologists, and resource economists was most useful and helpful to me. Third, several individuals have seen the need to support our interdisciplinary landscape research effort.

Three supporting agencies have funded the work upon which this study is based. Generous support was provided by the United States Department of Agriculture (USDA) Forest Service; the Pinchot Institute of Environmental Forestry Research, with the help of Dr. Shafer; and the United States Department of the Interior (USDI) Office of Water Resources, with the help of

Professor Bernard Berger. The most significant funding, however, came from the Massachusetts Agricultural Experiment Station, directed by Dr. Arless Spielman. Of his associates, Dr. William Mellen helped to provide our research team with initial funding, and more recently Dr. John Naegele has been especially helpful in significantly expanding our landscape research group.

Many of the assessment and planning techniques summarized here were developed by members and advisers of the landscape research team I established seven years ago. This team is usually referred to by its acronym "METLAND." Specific credit has already been given to those whose work appears within this book; moreover, their ideas in formal and informal communications have influenced my thinking throughout these years. Several of them commented on the manuscript, and many of their suggestions were included in this book. My sincere thanks go to Stephanie Caswell, Susan Cole, Donald Doehring, William Fahrer, Kimball Ferris, John Foster, Christopher Greene, William Hendrix, Spencer Joyner, and my colleague, Paul Procopio.

I received much direct help from Stephanie Caswell, Kimball Ferris, Ruth Laliberte, Frances Paulo, Richard Rosenthal, and Charles Yuill. For over a year, Frances Paulo served as my special assistant. In this capacity, she filled the many gaps in our landscape research reference library and compiled much of the material in the recommended reading list. Richard Rosenthal prepared all the graphics, thus substantially improving this book. Kimball Ferris and Stephanie Caswell did the initial editing of my first draft. Ruth Laliberte did all the typing and retyping of each of its versions. And Charles Yuill reviewed all the references used in the manuscript and expanded the recommended reading list. And finally, I wish to express a special note of gratitude to Christopher Greene, who edited this manuscript for me. To all of these friends and colleagues, I give my sincere thanks and full acknowledgment of my indebtedness.

Julius Gy. Fabos

PLANNING THE TOTAL LANDSCAPE: A GUIDE TO INTELLIGENT LAND USE

1 INTRODUCTION

One of the major ramifications of technological development over the past fifty years has been the complete transformation of the pattern of urban development in industrialized countries. Until the middle of this century, the expansion of cities generally concentrated more and more people and buildings around an important regional transportation node. In earlier times, this node might have been a natural harbor or a fordable stretch of river; later it was perhaps a railway depot or a stop on a trolley route. The availability of private automobiles, however, robbed these historical determinants of urban location of their force; not only could a car travel wherever there were roads, but it soon became evident that it was feasible, both technically and economically, to build roads to many more areas of the landscape than had been possible with any previous form of transport infrastructure. This fact has had particular significance in the areas near older urban concentrations. The "opening up" of the countryside has proved to be a tremendous stimulus to development as thousands of former city dwellers found in "suburban living" at least a simulacrum of rural amenity. For the first time in history, decentralization had become the model of urban growth.

The benefits of this new urban pattern, like most benefits, were won only at a cost. Most of the conversion of rural land from forests and farms to houses, shopping centers, and industrial parks has been haphazard and indiscriminate. As a result, the costs have mounted. The resources in the land have been degraded and destroyed. Natural hazards that previously occurred with little adverse effect—because no one was in their way—now result in billions of dollars worth of damage annually. Land is seldom used for the purposes for which it is inherently best suited. Finally, the synergistic effects of all human actions may impair the ecological balance. The consequences for future generations can only be guessed at.

For these reasons, many observers have suggested that large-scale urban decentralization may be the most important environmental problem of our time. In some areas, expanding metropolitan regions have grown so large that they have become contiguous, forming what the French geographer Jean Gottman has called a "megalopolis."[1] The first and most notorious megalopolis comprises the belt of urban and suburban development that stretches from Boston, Massachusetts, to Washington, D.C. By 1961, this region held more than thirty million people distributed over some sixty thousand square miles.

Most of the development decisions that have led to the current metropolitan "sprawl" have been based primarily on economic, political, and social factors. Many of the negative environmental effects resulting from this perspective would have been avoided if the inherent attributes of the land had been adequately considered in land use decision making.

The potential of landscape planning, as environmentally responsive land use planning is often called, is not a new notion. One early advocate for this approach was Benton MacKaye, an American forester. His book *The New Exploration: A Philosophy of Regional Planning,* published in 1928, included an eloquent warning on the dangers of the "metropolitan invasion."[2] MacKaye suggested that action should be taken to preserve major landscape features such as waterways and forested ridges to serve as "natural levees" against the flood of new development.

In large part, MacKaye's proposals form the conceptual basis of modern landscape planning. Many of the assessment techniques presented in this book merely extend the categories of landscape "features" that help to determine which areas of land should be preserved and which developed. There is, however, an additional issue, which although not addressed explicitly here nonetheless represents a critical conceptual facet of landscape planning. Namely, the benefits that are won (and the potential costs avoided) by considering environmental factors in land use decisions accrue to the population at large, in both present and future generations. For example, the protection of a local groundwater supply, which eliminates the need to import water from distant reservoirs, saves the community money and reduces the overall consumption of energy. In other words, land-based development decisions promote the *public good.* The problem is that in this country, a social norm identifies land and natural resources as private commodities. The "rights" of American property owners include the right to use land in ways that advance their own, *private good.* There is thus a conflict inherent in the proposition of landscape planning. Many planning measures proposed for the public good foundered on the rocks of the private right to anticipate and derive profits from land.[3]

Therefore, it is important that the improvements in the techniques of landscape assessment that are presented in the following chapters are seen as necessary for the prudent use of land to the maximum benefit of society. But these improvements are themselves not enough. Our general attitudes toward land ownership must likewise change if the promise of landscape planning is to be realized. This change has already taken place with respect to the commodities of water and air; we have come to regard them unequivocally as public goods. That land is also a public good is a notion accepted in some degree in virtually every other industrialized society. For efficient, equitable, and prudent land use to take place in our country, the legitimacy of land use regulation in the public good must be recognized here, too.

The reassertion of public versus private rights in land is in fact under way, albeit rather slowly. The federal government has enacted several pieces of legislation that mandate public intervention in private land use decision making, including the Water Pollution Control Act, as amended, in 1972 (PL 92-500) and the National Environmental Policy Act of 1969 (PL 91-190). Several states—such as Vermont, Maine, and Hawaii—have passed laws calling for the regulation of commercial, residential, and industrial development; these laws have been passed in response to a perceived threat to the quality of the general environment. Although most of these efforts have suffered some setbacks in implementation, the progress along this front is encouraging.

Parallel to these legislative developments, significant advances have occurred in the techniques of landscape assessment and planning during the past two decades. As discussed in this book, the field of landscape assessment and planning integrates three component processes. The most basic component is scientific knowledge, which helps to identify the significance and magnitude of resource, hazard, suitability, and ecological issues. One of the principal aims of this book is to present the current "state of the art" of scientifically based assessment procedures for various significant landscape factors.

The second component of landscape assessment and planning has to do with the ascription of qualitative values to the results of quantitative assessment procedures. For instance, a survey may locate several high-quality and abundant groundwater supply sites. But how can one determine the present and future value of those resources to society? So far, economic valuation procedures appear to be the most useful. By assigning a dollar value to a given amount of the resource, the value is at once consistent and easily comprehensible. In Part 3 of this book, some of the economic values of assessed landscape resources are presented. A detailed discussion of economic valuation procedures, however, will not be undertaken.

The third component of landscape assessment and planning includes the various systems of spatial data manipulation that can process, store, and retrieve information on one or more landscape parameters. Most of the assessment and planning examples shown in Parts 2 and 3 use recently developed geographic data manipulation systems. A general discussion of these techniques is presented in Chapter 4.

Much of the literature of landscape assessment and planning is highly technical. This technical information is of use primarily to environmental specialists and landscape planners. However, as we have seen, most decisions affecting urbanization are made by others. By presenting these various landscape assessment and planning approaches in a less technical manner, this book should bridge this unfortunate and largely unnecessary gap between the environmental specialists, on the one hand, and decision makers and the general public on the other.

PLAN OF THE BOOK

The text is divided into three parts. Part 1 deals with the emergence of the concept of landscape planning and discusses its increasing influence on planning in the metropolitan landscape. Part 2 describes some of the environmental landscape assessment techniques that have been developed during the past few decades. Part 3 presents some commonly used landscape planning techniques that have been developed to integrate and synthesize the results of the various individual assessment techniques described in Part 2. Part 3 also presents some of the emerging systems models that seem to have great potential in the area of landscape planning.

Because of lack of space, several topics related to environmental assessment and landscape planning have not been included in this survey: e.g.,the energy implications of landscape planning; the effects of pesticides and fertilizers on environmental quality; and the basic policy issues an application of the various assessment techniques would raise, such as how best to implement regulations.

NOTES

1. Jean Gottman, *Megalopolis: The Urbanized Northeastern Seaboard of the United States* (Cambridge, Mass.: MIT Press, 1961).

2. Benton MacKaye, *The New Exploration: A Philosophy of Regional Planning* (Urbana: University of Illinois Press, 1962).

3. C. Trillin, "250 and Beyond," *The New Yorker*, November 4, 1974, pp. 128-135.

PART 1

THE EMERGENCE OF LANDSCAPE CONCERN AND PLANNING TECHNIQUES

2 THE PROBLEMS OF METROPOLITANIZATION

The decentralized metropolis in its present form has been in existence for but a short time. Until 1945, even the largest urbanized areas covered only one or two hundred square miles. Their impact on the hinterlands was small. In the years after World War II, the size and configuration of the major metropolises in Europe and North America began to change. Industries and populations, released from their dependence on rail communications by the increasingly available automobiles, could locate their activities farther and farther from the urban centers.[1]

This rapid decentralization opened up many new opportunities for the burgeoning suburban population. For many people, the quality of life perceptibly improved. But with this growth came several problems associated with how the land was used. The creation of the suburban landscape proceeded with little understanding of the structure and function of the environment that supported it and, in most cases, with little concern for that environment.

The first part of this chapter discusses the evolution of the sprawling suburban landscape and describes its transformation from metropolis into megalopolis. The second part analyzes the landscape problems brought about by this process, focusing on the misuse of landscape resources, the generation of landscape hazards, the abuse of inherent suitability for development, and the impact on environmental quality in general.

BEFORE THE MEGALOPOLIS

The form and location of cities before industrialization were constrained by the natural characteristics of the land. Before the Industrial Revolution, nearly all major European towns and cities were located near good agricultural land and a natural transportation link, such as a secure overland route, a navigable river, or a protected harbor. The Italian cities of Venice, Genoa, Milan, and Florence, for example, owe their location and a large measure of their success to their proximity to the fertile plains of Lombardy and the Mediterranean Sea.

The density of these medieval and renaissance cities was high. Clough estimates that some of these cities held about 100,000 people by 1450.[2] In size, however, they seldom were larger than one or two square miles. This resulted in a density comparable to that of present-day Manhattan.

The size and density of the cities of Europe increased during the period 1300-1740, although urban growth before the Industrial Revolution was slow and incremental. The preindustrial expansion of Paris is shown in Figure 1. Three hundred years of steady growth were necessary for the city to grow from a size of one square mile in 1300 to three square miles in 1600. By 1740, the size of Paris had increased at a faster rate, but it still covered only about eight square miles.

The technological advances that permitted the densities of preindustrial cities such as Paris and Milan to become so high—such as development of three-story and four-story buildings[3]—of course did not solve all of the problems of urban life. Because of inadequate sanitation facilities, for instance, devastating epidemics occurred. The relatively small size of these cities, however, meant that their impact on the regional environment throughout the preindustrial period was marginal.

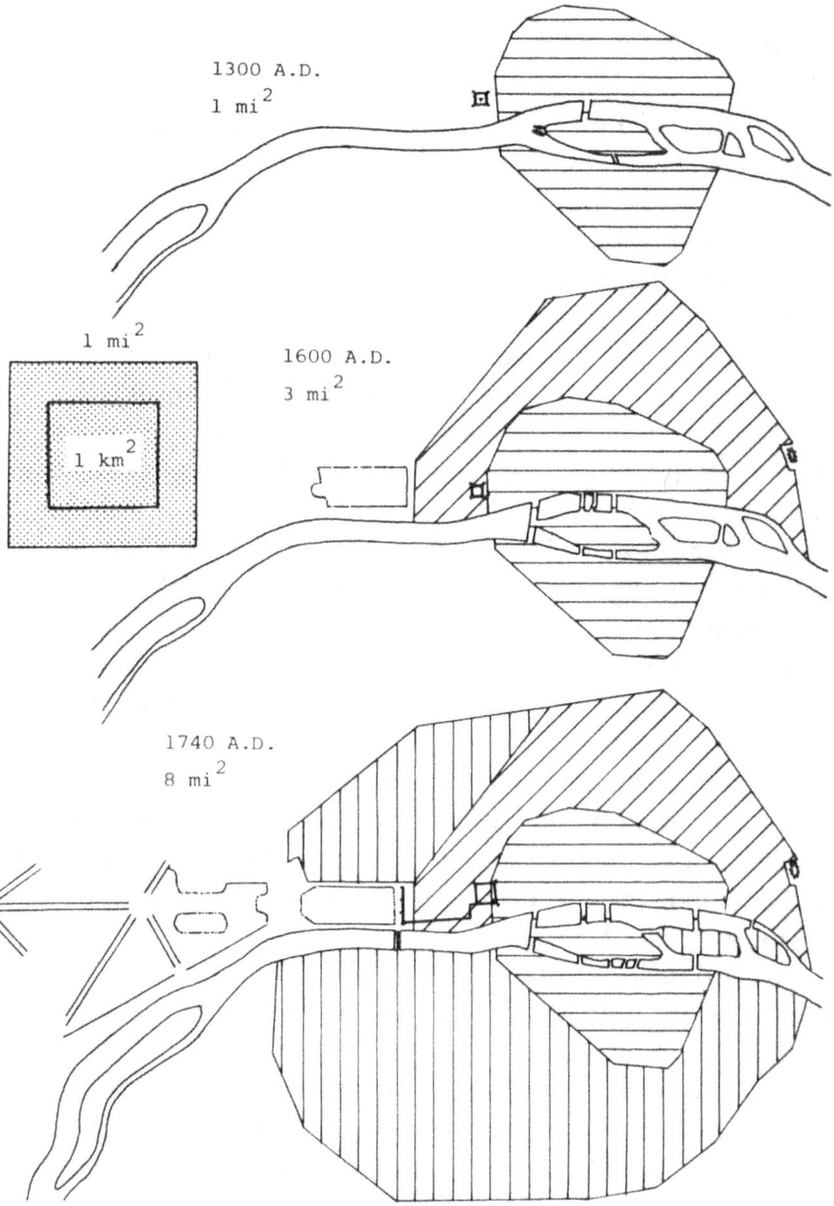

FIGURE 1. Paris from the Middle Ages to the dawn of the Industrial Revolution. During this period the city occupied a relatively small area when compared with present-day metropolitan Paris, which covers 125 square miles (325 square km).

A major change in the size and quality of cities occurred during the Industrial Revolution, as science and technology were applied to the exploitation of many primary energy resources and minerals, principally coal and iron. These developments, which occurred throughout Western Europe as well as in the United States, led to the creation of what Hoskins has called the "industrial landscape."[4] For the first time, it becomes possible to refer to urbanized regions, such as the Ruhr in Germany and the Liverpool-Manchester-Leeds belt in England. However, the environmental degradation that characterized this industrial landscape was confined mostly to the cities themselves. Most of the agricultural countryside remained relatively unsullied.

Industrialization, nonetheless, wrought three visible changes upon the patterns of urban land use. The first was the growth of totally new towns and cities adjacent to sources of the natural resources required by industrial processes. Preston, a mill town in northwestern England, was located amid the highly productive Lancashire coalfields. The growth of the textile industry, brought on in part by the ample coal supply, increased the population of Preston fifteenfold—from 6,000 in 1777 to more than 90,000 in 1877.[5]

The second change in land use patterns during this period was the development of new urban settlements in response to newly created transportation routes. First the canals and then the railroads allowed the urban development of lands that were previously "out of the way."

The third major change was the rapid enlargement of the older cities. The locational factors that had led to the founding of London and New York, for example—such as good harbors—became even more important during this era of trade. By the end of the nineteenth century, most of the large industrial metropolises were established. These major urban settlements, often more than a hundred square miles in extent, housed populations whose numbers were counted in millions (Figure 2).

In configuration, most of the new metropolises were star-shaped. Development took place along the radial railroad and

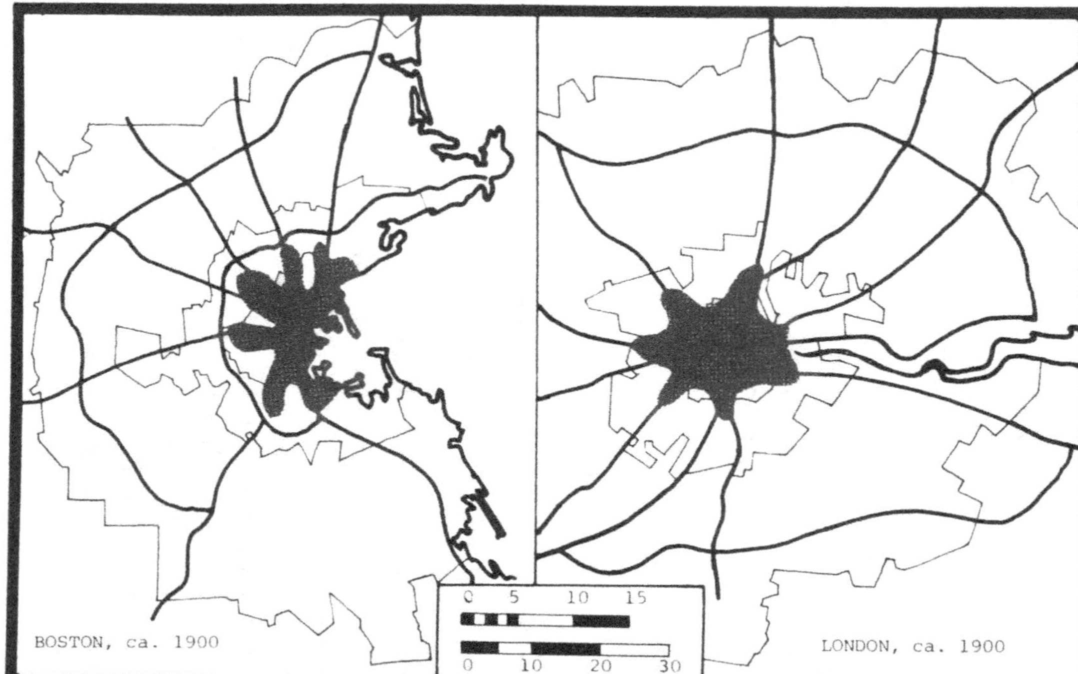

FIGURE 2. By 1900 the expansion of the industrial city was complete, forming large urban centers with populations of over 1 million. Development occurred along major transportation lines, as indicated by the shaded areas above, and often stretched out radially ten miles from the city center. The nineteenth-century industrial city occupied from five to ten times the densely populated area that Paris did at the beginning of the Industrial Revolution (see Figure 1). Note the strong similarities between London's development and that of Boston.

streetcar routes leading out of the centers of cities. Thus, even though by 1900 urban settlements had reached a scale greater than ever before, large wedges of agricultural or forested land between the railway corridors continued to escape the impact of urban growth.

The first signs of change in this pattern were evident by the 1920s and 1930s. The automobile, which unlike streetcars could go anywhere there were roads, made the interstices of the rail network easily accessible. And, as in the past, with access came development. At first, the conversion of the remaining countryside near the cities to residential use was limited to the "estates" of the upper class (Figure 3). The extensive environmental problems posed by the decentralized urban landscape of the present day had yet to appear.

MEGALOPOLIS AND BEYOND

If one flies from Washington, D.C., to Boston, Massachusetts, during the late evening, a terrestrial Milky Way of lights is seen throughout the entire region. These lights illuminate the buildings and roads of the "megalopolis"—a virtually unbroken fabric of interlocking cities and suburbs that extends for over four hundred miles along the northeastern seaboard. Geographer Jean Gottman first used the term *megalopolis* to describe this region; his important book *Megalopolis* (1961) is a detailed examination of the new urban pattern between Boston and Washington (Figure 4). As is clear from his analysis, the forces that brought about the rapid decentralized growth of this region can be found in many other areas throughout the industrialized world.

The megalopolitan form of development represents a major change in the evolution of cities. Until the twentieth century, as we have seen, increasing urbanization almost always meant larger and more centralized development, with little if any change in density. Access was always a controlling factor and it was almost always limited, first by how far one could walk and later by

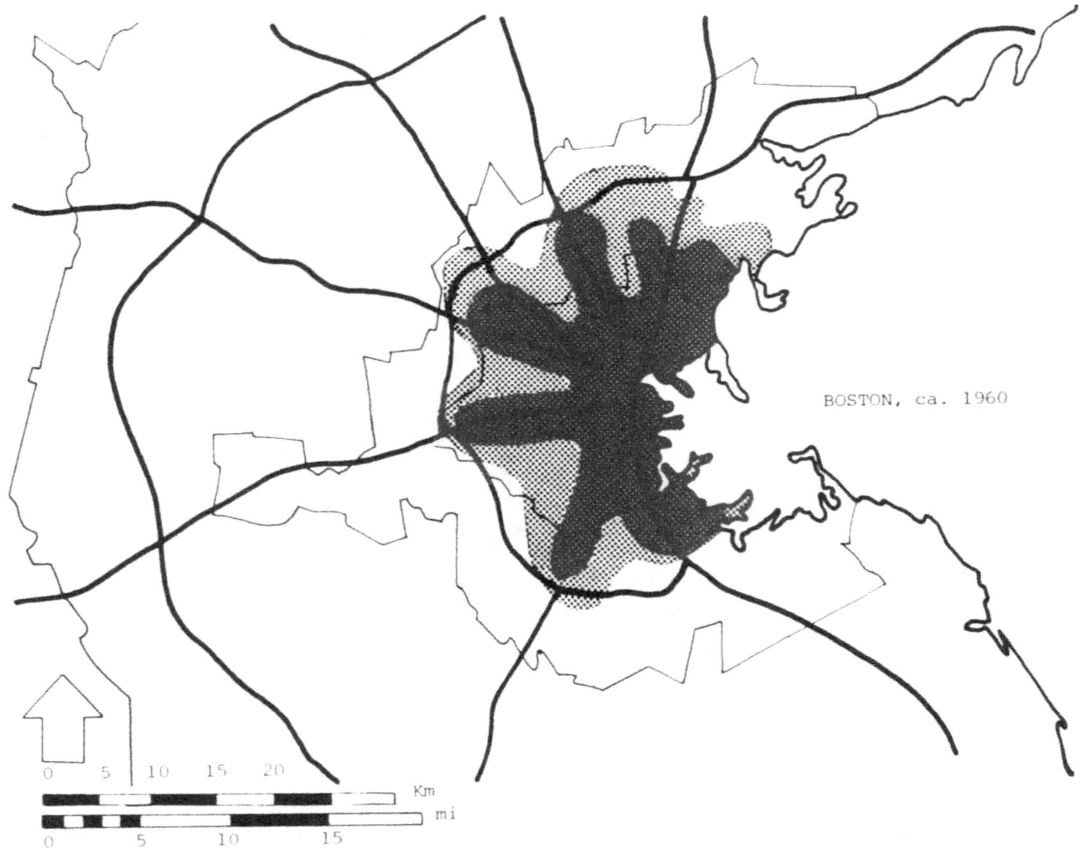

FIGURE 3. The automobile was primarily responsible for rapid urban incursions into the rural landscape. The darker tone represents a densely populated urban Boston ca. 1900. The lighter tone represents a decentralized urban Boston ca. 1960.

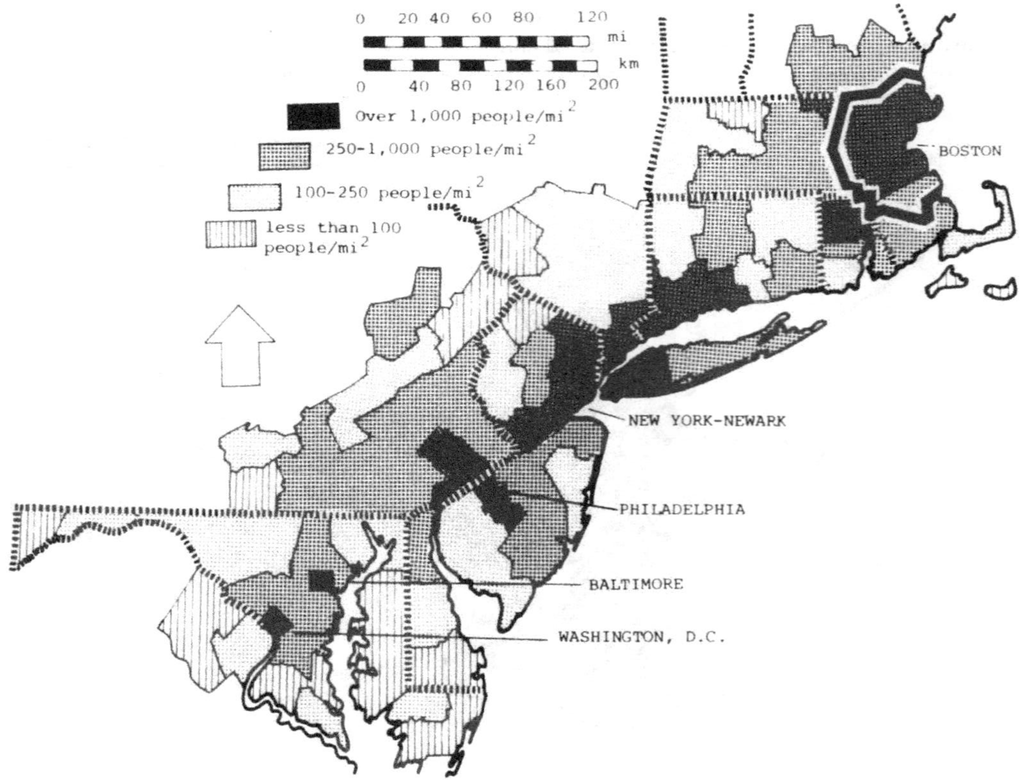

FIGURE 4. The rapid decentralization of the old urban centers—a post–World War II phenomenon—resulted in the development of the megalopolis. This illustration depicts the megalopolis of the eastern seaboard of the United States, identified and delineated by the French geographer Jean Gottman. (The Boston metropolitan region is outlined in heavy black.)

where the streetcars ran. The invention of the private automobile, which could provide access throughout a region, was the basic genesis of the change in land use. Although cars began to be used in the early 1900s, their impact on urban development was delayed by the two world wars and the Great Depression, periods when only the very affluent could afford cars. The impact of automobiles, however, was inevitable. With the relative prosperity of the Eisenhower years came tremendous increases in car ownership.[6] In the United States, the national highway-building program responded to the growth in the numbers of cars with a phenomenal expansion and improvement in the nation's road system, especially in the already populous Northeast. Of course, more cars also brought more congestion to the central cities and older suburbs, and many people were thus prompted to move to less crowded areas. The "countryside" meant the good life to the many middle-class families who now owned a car. And the new suburbs represented a chance to live in the countryside.

The governments of the industrialized countries responded to the pressures of decentralization in various ways. In Great Britain, for example, the notion of the "garden city," which Ebenezer Howard had expounded in the nineteenth century, was revived.[7] In 1946, the New Town Act was passed, which called for the concentration of new urban growth in discrete, higher-density towns located around the older cities but beyond a "greenbelt" of preserved agricultural land. This was followed in 1947 by the Town and Country Planning Act, which reduced the number of planning units and attempted to provide an adequate statutory frameword for metropolitan regional land use planning.[8] In spite of these measures, however, population densities have continued to decrease in the central cities and increase in the outskirts (Figure 5). Nonetheless, the British attempts appear to be far ahead of the U.S. response to the megalopolitan surge.

The answer to decentralization in land use in the United States and Canada over the last thirty years has for the most part been more decentralization. Part of this can be attributed to the great amounts of undeveloped land available in these areas. Whatever

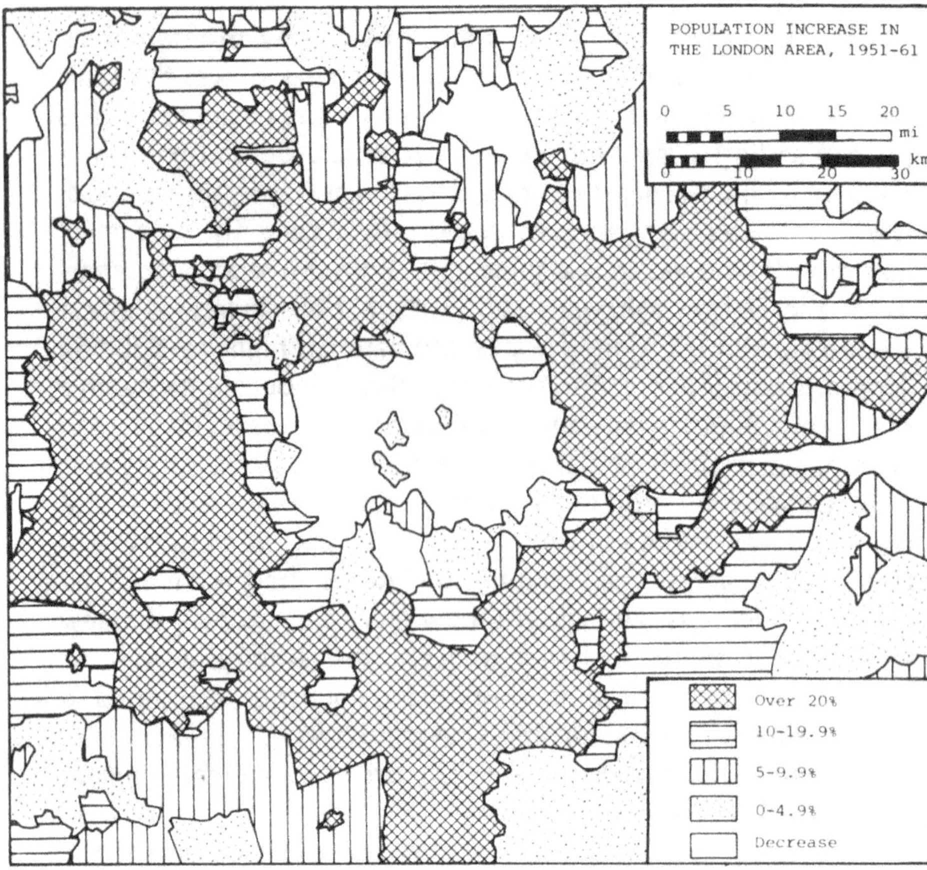

FIGURE 5. British efforts to stem suburban development and expansion met with limited success. The so-called Green Belt around London is almost congruent with the fastest growing region, as indicated by the crosshatch. In contrast, London proper suffered a decline in population, underscoring the shift from higher-density to lower-density settlement patterns discussed in the text.

the reason, it is clear that governmental policies, such as mortgage subsidies for home buyers and various tax loopholes, have encouraged millions of middle-class Americans to move to the suburbs.[9]

The effect of the highway program in stimulating suburban growth has already been mentioned. A case study of the Boston metropolitan region illustrates this phenomenon clearly. In 1950, Boston and its surrounding suburbs covered approximately 250 square miles, or roughly 3 percent of the land in Massachusetts. By

1952, one of the first major circumferential belt highways in the country—Route 128—was built around the perimeter of the existing suburbs. The purpose of this "miracle highway," as it was then called, was to ease congestion in the center of Boston and to provide easy car and truck access to additional land as a spur to economic development. Its success on the latter point is indisputable. Most of the towns traversed by Route 128 increased in population by 100-400 percent in ten years. Over the same period, the overall size of the Boston metropolitan region doubled, growing to 500 square miles. By the early 1960s, plans were announced for a second belt highway fifteen miles further out from Route 128. The completion ten years later of Interstate Route 495 has opened up an additional two thousand square miles for similar urban growth (Figure 6).[10]

The Boston metropolitan highway program is typical in its concentration on short-term traffic and economic goals. In their 1970 survey of metropolitan planning, Boyce, Day, and McDonald concluded that the transportation plans of seven major U.S. cities reflected primarily the input of highway engineers. The contributions of landscape architects or planners during the planning stage were in each case found to be insignificant or nonexistent.[11]

By 1975, when the major part of the U.S. superhighway construction program was complete, the context of urban land use had been drastically changed. In thirty years, the urbanized areas of the twenty-five largest metropolitan regions in the United States increased in size from five to ten times.[12] The areal extent of these regions now ranges from two thousand square miles around an isolated city to the nearly sixty thousand square miles of the Boston-to-Washington megalopolis.[13]

One final point should be made about megalopolitan growth. The development of the megalopolis has been referred to here as "urbanization," but the physical appearance of much of the region is far from urban in the traditional sense. Gottmann points out that the average population density of the Boston-Washington region is roughly one person per acre.[14] Since many of the 32 million residents of megalopolis in 1960 lived in the much denser older cities, it is easy to see that the density of many of the

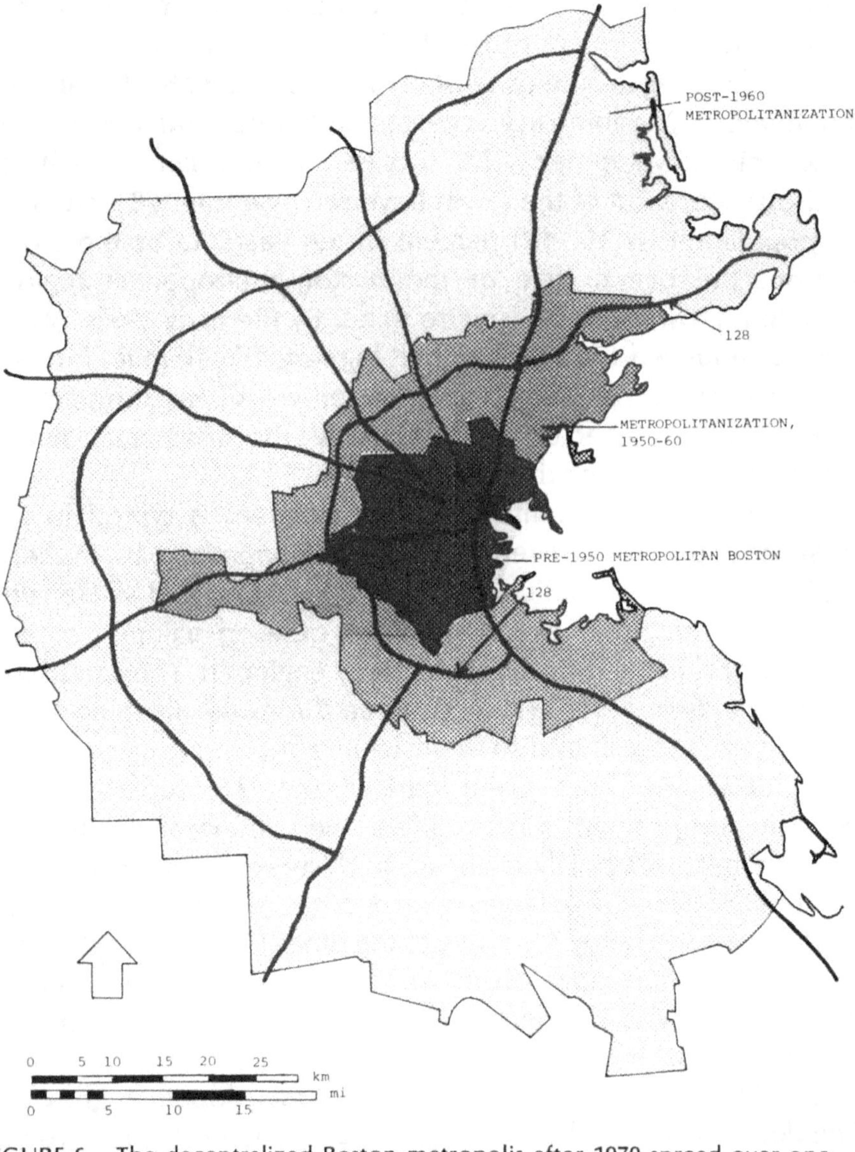

FIGURE 6. The decentralized Boston metropolis after 1970 spread over one-third of Massachusetts. This lower-density development has an impact on about 2,500 square miles of landscape. This area is fifty times larger than the Boston metropolis at the turn of the century.

FIGURE 7. A typical distribution of the dominant land use types in the megalopolitan region of the northeastern seaboard of the United States.

suburban areas is considerably lower than one person per acre. Gottman's figures show that in 1960 approximately half the land in the megalopolis was forested; an additional one-third was either tilled or grazed. Only 15 percent was actually devoted to buildings and roads.[15] An observer traveling through this megalopolitan region, therefore, sees a predominantly rural scene with an interspersion of varying densities of built-up land (Figure 7). But these are not hinterlands. They occupy the coastal plain east of the Appalachian Mountains and, as can be seen in Figure 8, occur primarily in landscapes with lower natural and cultural qualities.

FUTURE TRENDS IN URBANIZATION

The established trend toward the dispersal of new development appears to be here to stay, at least for the foreseeable future. This is not to say that the older central cities will not still serve many functions and in some cases become more densely populated. Rather, it reflects a conviction that many people and employers will continue to find suburban locations attractive and that with good highway access, growth in these areas is insured. This view is held in spite of the prognosis of serious energy shortages. The individualized, versatile transportation offered by automobiles will not easily be forsaken; neither will the enormous public investment in roads or the private profitability of automobile manufacturers. If gasoline becomes an unfeasible fuel, we may find that automobiles are powered by other fuels but powered they will be.

In Europe as well as in North America, therefore, the continued growth and merging of megalopolises seem inevitable. The Greek urban theorist Constantine Doxiadis has predicted that within a hundred years:

> the total population [of the earth] will be on the order of twenty to thirty billion, the urban population about twenty times larger than at present, the economic forces, the mechanics, the area of the human settlement almost terrifying. By then they will be all interconnected in total continuous universal settlement, into an ecumenic city or ecumenopolis, whose dimensions can be understood if we think that from Milwaukee to Chicago, Detroit, Cleveland, Buffalo, and beyond it to Toronto and up to the Atlantic, there will be a continuous city [see Figure 9].[16]

He might also have added an "ecumenopolis" stretching from Maine to Florida, where the developmental stimulus of Interstate Highway 95 has already begun.

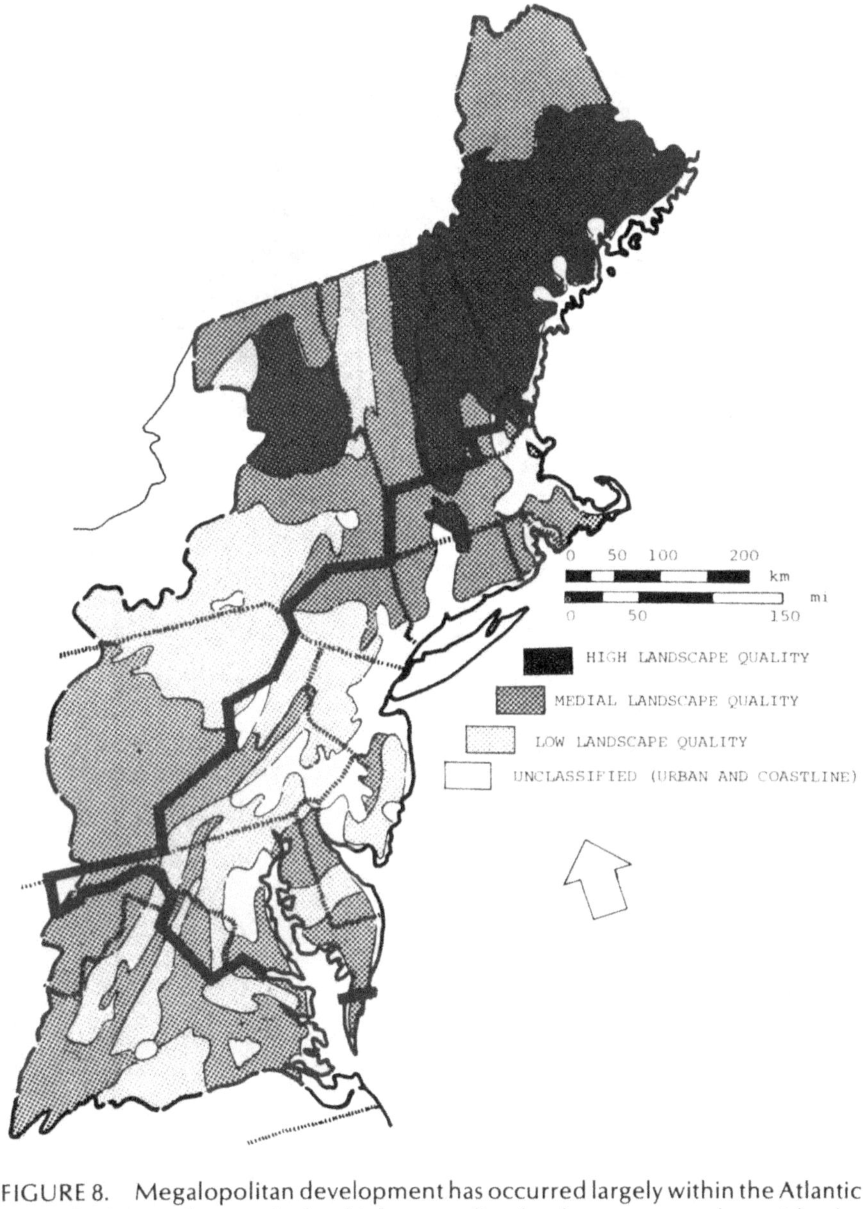

FIGURE 8. Megalopolitan development has occurred largely within the Atlantic Coastal Plain. Almost all the highest-quality landscapes spread outside the megalopolis (heavy black line).

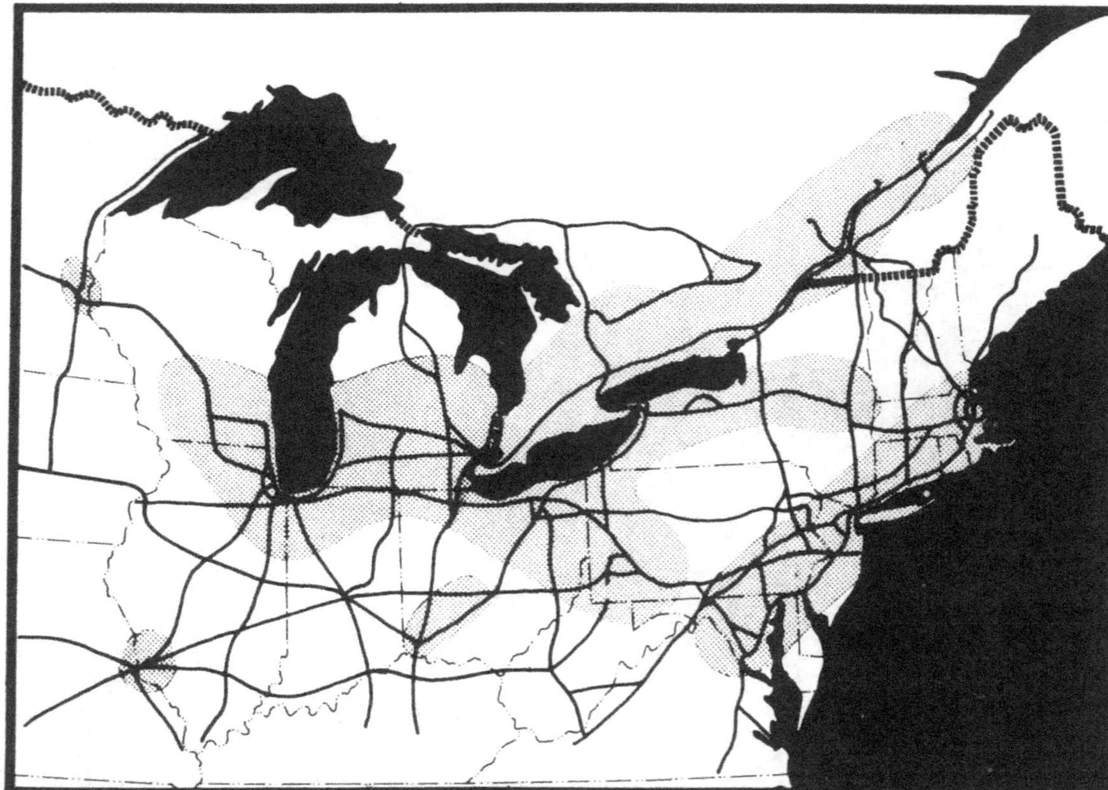

FIGURE 9. According to the Greek planner Doxiadis, the megalopolitan areas appear to be growing together along major transportation corridors. (The megalopolitan areas are shaded; the interstate highway system is shown by the heavy black lines.)

LANDSCAPE PROBLEMS ASSOCIATED WITH METROPOLITANIZATION

The rapid, uncontrolled growth of our urban regions offers a number of benefits to the people involved, as we have seen. But in their attention to the limited issues of transportation and short-term economic gains, the shapers of this development pattern—public planners and private developers alike—have seen the landscape as a commodity with one dimension: location. Almost any land that is fortuitously situated from the point of view of a given use has been considered "developable." The landscape, however, has various attributes that are germane to its use, including its inherent suitability for development, its resource potential, and its susceptibility to hazards. These characteristics can significantly affect the overall success of urban development. All too often they are either imperfectly understood or ignored.

The misuse of landscape resources and the unnecessary exposure of human settlements to hazard is not a new phenomenon. In southern Europe, for example, extensive evergreen and oak forests were cut down centuries ago. Because of the relatively hot and dry climate of that region, these indigenous forests were unable to regain a foothold and have never renewed themselves.[17] The problem was exacerbated by the overgrazing of livestock on the denuded hillsides, which accelerated the widespread erosion that characterizes the area to this day.

A most dramatic illustration of persistent inattention to important landscape characteristics was documented by Klein in his study of flooding in Florence, Italy. While investigating the disastrous flood of 1966, Klein found that "since 1333 there has been a moderate flood of the Arno river and a massive flood every 100 years. Of the massive floods, those of November, 1333; November, 1844; and November, 1966, have been the worst. Since 1500 there have been more than 50 floods qualifying as moderate and 54 qualifying as major."[18]

The flood disasters of Florence can be related to two factors.

First, the original location of Florence—on the wet, marshy banks of the Arno—was poor. Second, since nearly all of the natural vegetation in the Arno watershed had been destroyed by the Middle Ages, the heavy rains that hit the Tuscan region each fall stripped millions of tons of soil from the hills and deposited them on the floodplain. The annual deposition of silt gradually filled in the original floodway and extended the limits of the floodplain, thereby increasing the hazard. Although this causative relationship is predictable, the residents of Florence have always been shocked anew with each recurring flood.

The insensitivity of the Florentines to the functioning of their environment is far from unique. In America, the European colonists burned most of the forests in New England to acquire more farmland. By the middle of the nineteenth century, several communities whose land had originally been covered by trees were importing wood for building from upstate New York. A more recent and somewhat more notorious example of the mismanagement of U.S. landscape resources led to the Dust Bowl. Here, the application of monocultural agricultural techniques propelled the dry Oklahoma grassland soils into oblivion in the space of thirty-five years.

Darling and Boyd document a comparable transmogrification of the Scottish Highlands.[19] Incremental destruction of the ancient forest by the eighteenth century brought about the erosion of virtually all of the fertile topsoil. Finally, only the lime-loving plants of the upland heath could survive, and they soon became the dominant species of the region.[20] The lowlands of Britain also suffered from insensitive use. Draining and farming in the coastal marshland known as the Bedford Levels (near Peterborough) in the seventeenth and eighteenth centuries made the peat level drop some twenty feet.[21]

In fact, instances of human misuse and mismanagement of landscape resources have been recorded thousands of times in books, articles, and even films. Yet this overwhelming body of evidence has not significantly altered our cultural norms. We continue to eliminate or pollute such essential and renewable resources as water, which must be imported over long distances at great costs in dollars and in energy. We blithely continue to build in flood-prone areas. With the aid of so-called technological advances in construction techniques, we now develop much "unsuitable" land despite its natural limitations. Billions of tons of earth are moved each year to fill in marshes or flatten hills.

The point is that we *do* have the means to avoid these mistakes. Most of these problems can be minimized if the resource, hazard, and suitability factors of the landscape are taken into consideration *before* development. The rest of this chapter is devoted to an exploration of each of these factors. In addition, the general long-term effects of human activity on the ecological functioning of the environment are also discussed.

LANDSCAPE RESOURCES

Consider the following fable. A man who owned a hundred acres of land was approached by a prospective buyer. "I'll give you five hundred dollars an acre for that land," the buyer said. Because $50,000 was somewhat more than the current market price for his land and was, at any rate, a good deal more than he had paid for it, the owner agreed to the sale. He gratefully accepted the money and moved into an apartment in town, pleased with his windfall profit. Several months later, however, his pleasure turned to dismay when a front-page story in the local paper informed him that a major oil field had been discovered under his farmland.

The hero of this parable (perhaps antihero is more appropriate) did not know the true market value of his property because he was *uninformed* about the resources it held. His private decision making about the use of that land is thus analogous to much of the public decision making that has accompanied the metropolitan and conversion process in recent years. The main difference is that our landowner learned of his mistake. Most communites rarely know what resources they are losing when acre upon acre of land is traded off for development. The costs of uninformed land use decisions are usually deferred; no doubt several years go by before a town finds out that it must import its drinking water because its local sources are insufficient or polluted. The public seldom understands the basic cause of the new tax hike necessitated by the water department's bigger budget—namely, that in a real sense, they themselves are at the root of the problem.

Landscape resources are useful and finite attributes of the environment. They are like money held in the bank: they are available for human use, but their scarcity requires that some mechanism define the objectives of their use and then allocate them in accordance with those objectives. Planning is one type of mechanism for facilitating these tasks, and adequate planning must be predicated on an understanding of the characteristics of the resources themselves.

Economists often divide natural resources into two categories: "flow" resources and "stock" resources. Flow resources are naturally self-renewing, as long as their renewal processes are not interfered with. Water is perhaps the most common flow resource. Stock resources, on the other hand, are depletable. Deposits of sand and gravel represent a significant stock resource in the metropolitan landscape.

A third category recognized by many landscape architects and planners is the so-called cultural resources. These include landscape attributes that take on value as a result of various cultural or societal norms. They may be either renewable or depletable. Aesthetic landscape resources, such as culturally valued panoramic views, are to some extent analogous to "flow" resources in that an obliterated view can sometimes be restored. However, there is usually little likelihood that an aesthetic resource will be rehabilitated after it has been degraded, and the ability of the landscape to renew its social attractiveness on its own (by vegetational succession, for example) may be a long-term process. For this reason, many analysts treat visual quality, together with other cultural resources such as historic sites, as irreplaceable stock resources.

Of the several flow resources likely to be important in

metropolitan areas, *water* is perhaps the most essential. There are generally two alternatives for supplying drinking water to a community. One is to impound water in an upland river or stream basin in order to form an artificial reservoir from which water is then carried by pipe to the distribution system. The watersheds of such reservoirs ideally include little or no urban development nor even large-scale agriculture so as to reduce the risk of polluted runoff flowing into the reservoir.

The second method is to extract water from porous, subterranean geologic formations known as aquifers. Groundwater aquifers are especially widely distributed in landscapes that were once covered by ice sheets. In such areas, they are often found in low-lying ground and are often much closer to urban settlements than the upland reservoir sites are. The water stored in aquifers either filters down through overlying permeable layers of rock or flows in at the point where the porous formation itself intersects the surface of the ground. Land in which either of these conditions occurs is known as an "aquifer recharge area." The geologic techniques for identifying potential aquifers and aquifer recharge areas are well developed. However, most of the rapid post–World War II metropolitan expansion has not taken such information into account. As a result, many hundreds of square miles of aquifer recharge areas have been built over. The deleterious effect of this is twofold. First, much urban development produces pollutants, which can contaminate a groundwater supply. These include harmful biological organisms from septic systems, salt from roads, and nonbiodegradable chemicals. Second, the rainwater that falls on many roofs and roads is channeled through storm sewers into rivers, thus reducing the volume of water that is "recharged" into an aquifer. So when development occurs over an aquifer—even if the water in the aquifer does not become polluted—the aquifer usually holds less water.

A second significant resource likely to be found in metropolitanizing regions is *biological productivity*. Trees, crops, wildlife, livestock—all depend on the land for the necessary conditions of life. Soil scientists have developed detailed techniques for analyzing the constituent elements of soils and assessing their relative productivity. The soils with the highest natural productivity contain a large amount of organic humus; they hold moisture well and are flat, well-drained, and free from stones or bedrock outcrops. Soils with all of these attributes are relatively rare: of the 465 million acres of cropland in the United States, only 72 million occur on Class I soil, as defined by the Soil Conservation Service. However, nearly half of the 72 million Class I acres are *within metropolitan regions.*[22]

The development pressures on productive land in expanding areas are particularly high. This is because many of the characteristics that make land suitable for farming, such as flatness and absence of stones, also mean that it can be built on with a minimum of physical constraints. In fact, the conversion of prime agricultural land to urban uses has reached significant proportions. Every year for the past twenty-five an average of over a million acres of farmland in the United States has been developed.

Agricultural productivity, however, is not the only productive potential of land that has been steadily destroyed by unplanned metropolitan growth. The potential to provide food and habitat for many forms of wildlife has also suffered, especially in the wetlands—both inland and coastal. The filling or draining of marshes and swamps is a time-honored "development" activity, even though wetlands are among the most productive of all ecosystems.

The second general category of resources includes the stock, or nonrenewable, resources. Most of the substances that come to mind when one mentions "natural resources" probably fall into this category: gold, iron, copper, fossil fuels, etc. Most of these resources, however, are usually not located in the path of suburban expansion. One group of stock resources that does occur in metropolitan regions and indeed is a necessary raw material for urban expansion is sand and gravel. Used in the fabrication of concrete, asphalt, and mortar, both sand and gravel are consumed in great quantities by construction contractors.

Natural deposits of these materials are generally well distributed, especially in glaciated landscapes. However, because their location is usually not immediately apparent to the untrained eye, many sand and gravel deposits are rendered unusable by the development of the land on top of them. The required supplies must therefore be transported from greater and greater distances, at substantial costs in energy as well as in dollars. There is little danger of an absolute shortage of sand and gravel, as there might be with, say, oil or natural gas. The problem here is that the cheap, easily accessible sources will be unnecessarily removed from consideration by imcompatible overlying or adjacent land uses. This is all too common in many urban areas but could be easily avoided if the sand and gravel sites of an area were systematically assessed before it is developed and if measures were introduced that are aimed at preserving them.

The third category—"cultural" resources—has also been needlessly degraded or lost in the course of urban expansion. This is, of course, also by no means a new phenomenon. The dense growth of the older central cities of Europe and the United States often completely obliterated all natural scenery. The urban park movement reflected a desire to reintroduce a bit of nature into cities where the original landscape had been destroyed.[23] However, the failure to assess the visual quality of a landscape before its development continues today just as it did in the past. We are often content to try to re-create culturally attractive areas after we have ruined them. A classic instance of this expensive (and usually unsuccessful) syndrome can be seen in Hartford, Connecticut. Located on the western bank of the Connecticut River, Hartford allowed virtually all of its scenic views and access to this scenic waterfront to be blocked by a series of superhighways. There, in 1962, at a cost of twenty-five dollars per square foot, Constitution Plaza—complete with elaborate gardens and water fountains—was built atop a parking garage.[24] This was as unnecessary as it was irresponsible. As with the other resources discussed above, the distribution and quality of aesthetic and cultural amenities must be assessed *before* the damage is done.

LANDSCAPE HAZARDS

The power of natural forces has been recognized throughout human history. The ancient Egyptians, for instance, understood that the autumn floods that replenished their soils would also destroy their settlements if they did not build on higher ground. However, many of the extreme events of nature are less predictable than the annual Nile floods. Even with modern scientific techniques, we still cannot predict with precision when and where a tornado will occur or where lightning will strike. Still, society is not totally at the mercy of these unpredictable environmental forces, for the techniques of anticipating the *relative likelihood* of their occurrence are available if we want to use them. Geologic faults have been mapped and monitored: we know where earthquakes are most likely to occur. The records of previous flooding on most major streams have been kept for many years: we know where floods are most likely to occur. The same is true for landslides, subsidence, coastal erosion, avalanches, and many other landscape hazards. The difficulty is that although we are often able to say with certainty that a given hazard will occur at a given site, at some time in the future, we cannot say exactly when. For most people, this kind of probabilistic warning has not deterred them from developing in hazard-prone areas. As a result of the continued development in floodplains, for instance, the annual losses to property alone from floods has risen to nearly $2 billion—even though over $9 billion has been spent since 1936 on public works aimed at controlling floodwaters.

Floods, earthquakes, and the other landscape hazards mentioned so far are essentially natural phenomena (although as will be seen below, human activities often exacerbate their impact). A second category of landscape hazards in metropolitan regions is essentially cultural (i.e., human-caused). This category includes several of the environmental by-products of technological development: air, water, and noise pollution. Unlike most natural hazards, whose occurrence cannot be prevented, the so-called cultural hazards of pollution can be eliminated, but only at a price. It is likely that a society will seek to balance the costs of reducing pollution (whether those costs are borne by the public or private sectors) against the option of protecting or shifting the adversely affected recipients. If land uses sensitive to noise, for instance, are simply not located within earshot of a noise source, then there is less need for noise attenuation at that source. Of course, this assumes that there is enough land to allow some flexibility in the distribution of land uses, a condition that does not usually occur in older, denser cities, but is more likely to exist in the developing suburban regions of a metropolis.

As with landscape resources, the prospect of planning urban growth with reference to hazards must be based on an adequate understanding of the significant hazards and their characteristics. Of the so-called natural hazards, floods are probably the most common within metropolitan regions of North America. The overflow of local water sources in average years is usually rather well known in most towns and cities, and provisions are made to protect lives and property from this "normal" flood level. The problem with floods, however, is that they periodically reach extraordinarily large proportions as a result of early snow melts, hurricanes, and other climatic irregularities. These floods are often referred to by the estimated frequency of their occurrence. Thus, we often hear of a "fifty-year flood" or a "hundred-year flood." These are floods whose level is reached or exceeded on an average of once every fifty or one hundred years. Of course there is nothing to prevent two fifty-year floods from occurring in consecutive years. A major flood of the Connecticut River in 1936 was followed by an equally large flood only two years later when a devastating hurricane hit New England.

Because of the relative infrequency of major floods in a given locale, growing communities have generally disregarded the risk from such floods. As a result, increased development occurs in the floodplain, thus raising the severity of the damage when a flood disaster strikes. However, urban development has other, less obvious impacts on flood hazards. The first of these is the "channelization" of the floodplain. When areas that would ordinarily be inundated are protected by artificial embankments or dikes, the stream flow is restricted. Since in periods of flooding the restricted flow will back up, this means that adjacent upstream lands become subject to a much greater flood hazard. In the view of Morgan, whose book *Dams and Other Disasters* examines the effect of physical flood control devices, these traditional cures have been worse than the disease.[25]

A second effect of urban development on riverine flooding is less obvious. It has been understood for several years that the impermeable nature of roofs and pavements in urban areas can decrease the amount of water stored in underground aquifers. A recent study of river basins in the Boston metropolitan region has found that urban development similarly inhibits the natural absorption of floodwaters.[26] As a result, the magnitude of any given flood is increased. In several basins in which considerable metropolitan expansion had occurred in the floodplain between 1952 and 1972, flood levels that had previously been reached or exceeded only once every hundred years could now be expected to occur once every *twenty* years. Moreover, the area of land now prone to inundation by the hundred-year flood has increased substantially as a consequence.

It seems clear from the evidence, then, that urban development on the floodplain land not only subjects that development to the hazard of flooding; it also places in jeopardy many areas that previously were relatively "safe."[27] In this context, the current interest in preserving wetlands for flood control because of their "spongelike" characteristics is encouraging. The federal initiative in restricting future floodplain development in the United States, as embodied in the National Flood Insurance Program, is a similar useful step.

Flooding is clearly the most widespread landscape hazard in metropolitan regions. However, several other hazards, though distributed much less evenly, have considerable local significance. Landslides, for instance, occur on certain unstable conditions, such as the colluvial deposits of rock and soil at the base of an eroded cliff. The foothills around Los Angeles, California, are notoriously susceptible to mud or landslides, yet these slopes are so scenic that wealthy Californians use them as homesites, a use that has occasionally led to disaster (Figure 10).[28]

The caving in, or subsidence, of the surface of the ground is usually limited to areas of porous, soluble bedrock, such as limestone. In several areas in Florida, subsidence is a potentially serious hazard. The problem can also be generated by mining activity—either directly, when the overburden collapses onto excavated space below the ground, or indirectly, as when the whole town of Germistown in South Africa caved in after the acid wastewater from local mining had dissolved the supporting rock.[29]

Earthquakes are a much less frequent hazard than floods, but when they do occur in inhabited areas, they bring severe devastation. The uncertainty of exactly where and when they will occur has led to unrestrained urban development in areas of even the most well known seismic risk. In fact, many of the fastest growing metropolitan regions in North America—including Boston, Montreal, and Seattle as well as Los Angeles and San Francisco—are located in areas of moderate to severe earthquake hazard (Figure 11).

Of the social "cultural" hazards that occur in urban regions, the most ubiquitous is air pollution. Generated by industrial processes, motor vehicle exhaust, and even home heating, air pollutants can usually be found in any urbanized area. The damage from this hazard is less catastrophic than that from most natural hazards since it occurs gradually. But the magnitude of its effects is equally great. There is more and more evidence that global and local changes in climate are linked to the chronic pollution of the atmosphere.[30] The detrimental effects on individual health and on inert materials are also well documented. The severity of air pollution, however, is not equally distributed throughout metropolitan regions. Local meteorological patterns, topography, and land use affect the concentrations of pollutants in the air.[31] The same is true for the often serious problem of excessive noise.[32] For both of these cultural hazards, then, one approach to the amelioration of their direct impact would be to assess the location

FIGURE 10. In Southern California, mud flows such as shown in this illustration are a frequent occurrence. Houses in the path of the mud slide are often filled with sediment or even swept along in the slide.

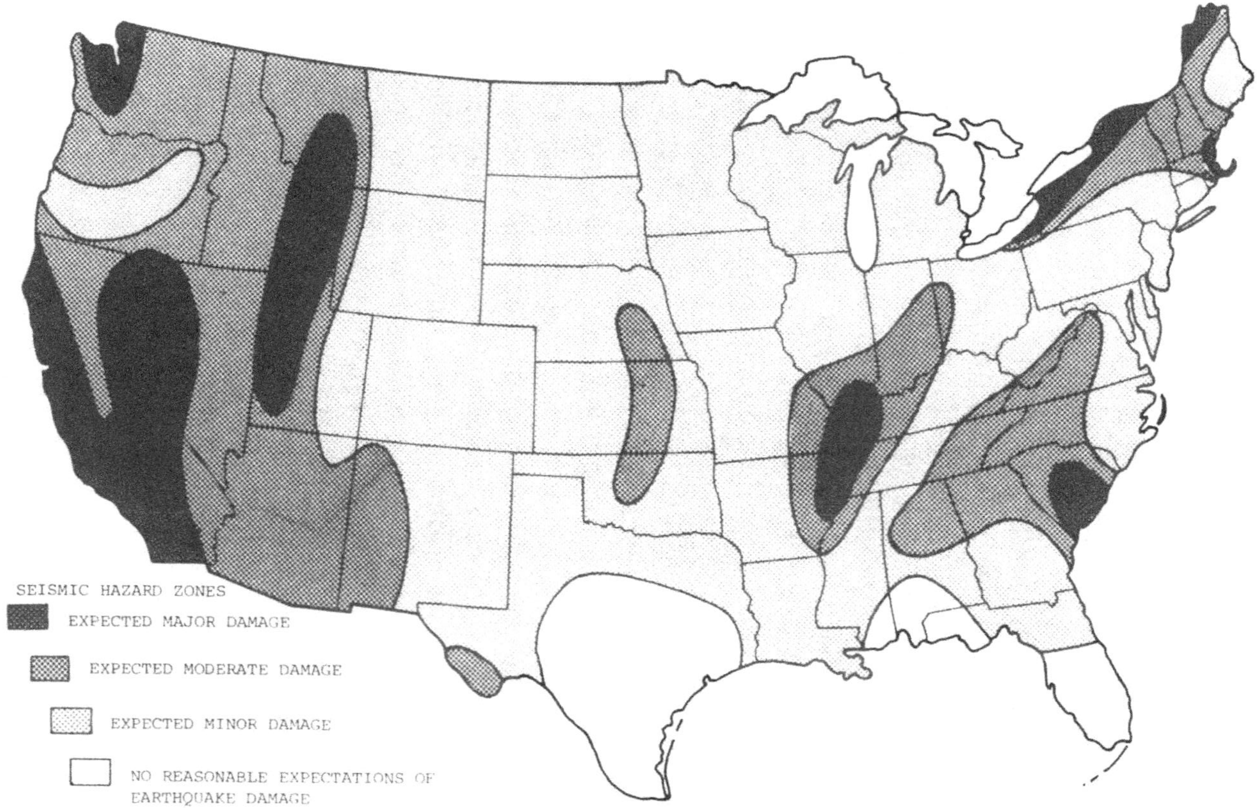

FIGURE 11. Some of the most important urban centers of North America are located in seismically hazardous regions. The best-known examples are San Francisco and Los Angeles; also on the danger list, however, are San Diego, Seattle, Buffalo, Montreal, Toronto, and Boston.

where the air and noise pollution is likely to be high and to direct sensitive new development to areas where the risk from these "hazards" is low.

DEVELOPMENT SUITABILITY

Advancements in construction technology have made it routinely possible to overcome many natural site constraints that in the past would have made development too difficult or too expensive. When virtually any site becomes developable in engineering terms, "accessibility" often becomes the prime determinant of what is the "highest and best use" of the land. This logic is reasonable, as far as it goes, but it does not go far enough. For example, suppose that the developer of an industrial park has a choice between two alternative sites. One site is a wetland that would need to be filled to a depth of eight feet before construction, but that is located next to the exit of an interstate highway. The second site would have minimum site preparation costs, but the closest major road to the property is two miles away. The first site is the obvious choice for development in spite of its inherent drawbacks. The cost of establishing transportation access is far higher than that of obtaining and depositing suitable fill material. The location of highway infrastructure is therefore of tremendous importance. Since development will usually occur where the highways are located, care should be taken to locate them in areas that will be suitable for the additional development they will generate.

Unfortunately, highways and highway exits are not located with the development suitability of the surrounding land in mind. The two belt highways around Boston (Figure 6) illustrate this point. Over 30 percent of the landscape between the highways consists of wetlands and floodplains. According to highway planners, however, some 80 percent of that landscape is developable.[33]

At least three significant factors make land suitable or unsuitable for conventional suburban development. The most obvious factor is the physical condition of the land itself. High water table, shallow bedrock, steep slopes, and poor bearing capacity—all combine to increase the costs of construction and often present long-term maintenance difficulties as well.

The second factor of development suitability that is nearly always overlooked in conventional land use planning is related to local climatic variation. Studies have shown that differences in how much sunlight reaches a site during colder periods can make a perceptible difference in the heating requirements of that site.[34] Winds are also important as a chilling factor in the winter and as a moderating influence in the summer. However, we have for the most part been content to depend on artificial heating and cooling to overcome microclimatic constraints and make up for lost microclimatic opportunities. The natural advantages of land that receives a fair amount of sun and is protected from winter winds are likely to become increasingly important, however, as we seek to conserve wasted energy on the one hand and to exploit the potential of solar energy on the other.

The third component of development suitability deals with aesthetic amenity. The attraction of people to areas of natural scenic beauty has been part of western culture at least since the dawn of Romanticism. There is concrete evidence that the presence of scenic views and mature trees tends to add significantly to the price people are willing to pay for a housing site.[35] Yet, again, the amenity value of land is seldom considered when major land use decisions are made in metropolitan communities.

In summary, the concept of development suitability implies that land has inherent opportunities as well as constraints. In its attention to areas where urban land use objectives can be met with the least impediment, development suitability assessment is an essential prescriptive focus for landscape planning. As such, it complements the basically proscriptive impulse that motivates the assessment of resources and hazards.

HUMAN IMPACT ON THE ENVIRONMENT

All three of the landscape attributes discussed so far—resources, hazards, and development suitability—reflect a fragmented analysis of the environment. Land is broken down into separately considered facets: wildlife productivity, groundwater potential, flood hazard potential, and so on. In addition, this analysis asks about the impact of environmental characteristics on the conduct of human activities. But the integrated, interrelated functioning of the environment has been conclusively demonstrated. There is a need to consider the landscape as a *holistic* system, a need the three components so far described do not satisfy.[36] And the central question must be reversed: what is the impact of human activity on the functioning of the environment?

Unfortunately, it is in this area of landscape analysis that we possess the least understanding. The evidence that the balance of many of our natural systems is being upset by dint of human action becomes more compelling with each report of a eutrophied lake or a decline in bird populations due to insecticide residue. But our sense of the complexity of environmental systems is increasing as well.

Landscape planning's role in reducing the uncertainties of environmental impact, for current and future generations alike, is perhaps one of its most significant potentials. How this and its other potentials can be realized is the central focus of this book. The next chapter describes the evolution of guiding principles that are proposed as a foundation from which landscape planning can move toward this goal.

NOTES

1. Jean Gottman, *Megalopolis: The Urbanized Northeastern Seaboard of the United States* (Cambridge, Mass.: MIT Press, 1961).
2. S. B. Clough, *The Economic Development of Western Civilization*, rev. ed. (New York: McGraw-Hill, 1959), p. 87.
3. A. B. Gullion and S. Eisner, *The Urban Pattern*, 2d ed. (Princeton,

N.J.: Van Nostrand, 1963), p. 40.

4. W. G. Hoskins, *The Making of the English Landscape* (Baltimore: Penguin Books, 1970), pp. 211-232.

5. Ibid., p. 228.

6. J. K. Galbraith, *The Affluent Society* (New York: Houghton Mifflin, 1958).

7. E. Howard, *Garden Cities of To-morrow* (London: Faber and Faber; Cambridge, Mass.: MIT Press, 1965).

8. D. Thomas, *London's Green Belt* (London: Faber and Faber, 1970), pp. 62-63.

9. C. M. Haar, *Land-Use Planning: A Casebook on the Use, Misuse, and Re-Use of Urban Land* (Boston: Little, Brown, 1971), Chapter 7.

10. J. Gy. Fabos, *Model for Landscape Resource Assessment,* Research Bulletin no. 602, University of Massachusetts, Agricultural Experiment Station, Amherst, Massachusetts (1973), pp. 7-21.

11. D. E. Boyce, N. D. Day, and C. McDonald, *Metropolitan Plan Making,* (Philadelphia, Pa.: Regional Science Research Institute, 1970).

12. Ibid.

13. H. Blumenfeld, "The Modern Metropolis," *Scientific American* 213, no. 3 (September 1965): 64-74.

14. Gottman, *Megalopolis,* p. 26.

15. Ibid., p. 234.

16. C. A. Doxiadis, *Between Dystopia and Utopia* (Hartford, Conn.: Trinity College Press, 1966).

17. H. C. Darby, "The Clearing of the Woodland in Europe," in *Man's Role in Changing the Face of the Earth,* ed. W. L. Thomas (Chicago: University of Chicago Press, 1956), p. 183.

18. R. M. Klein, "The Florence Flood," *Natural History* 77, no. 7 (August-September 1969): 54.

19. F. F. Darling and J. M. Boyd, *The Highlands and Islands* (London: Collins, 1964), pp. 55-57.

20. S. T. Eyre, *Vegetation and Soils: A World Picture* (Chicago: Aldine Publishing Co., 1963), pp. 176–180.

21. Ibid., pp. 190-191.

22. R. F. Dickinson, "The Process of Urbanization," in *Future Environments of North America* (Garden City, N.Y.: Natural History Press, 1966), pp. 463-678.

23. J. Gy. Fabos, G. T. Milde, and V. M. Weinmayr, *Frederick Law Olmsted, Sr.: Founder of Landscape Architecture in America.* (Amherst, Mass.: University of Massachusetts Press, 1968), pp. 17-42.

24. Fabos, *Model for Landscape Resource Assessment,* pp. 51-52.

25. A. E. Morgan, *Dams and Other Disasters: A Century of the Army*

Corps of Engineers in Civil Works (Boston: Sargent, 1971).

26. J. Gy. Fabos, "Are We Building on Flood Plains? Some Findings of the METLAND Study," *Findings* (Massachusetts Agricultural Experiment Station, Amherst, Massachusetts) May-June 1974, pp. 4-5.

27. L. B. Leopold, "Hydrology for Urban Land Planning," in *Man and His Physical Environment: Readings in Environmental Geology* (Minneapolis: Burgess Publishing Co., 1972).

28. N. T. Kenney, "Southern California's Trial by Mud and Water," *National Geographic Magazine* 36 (October 1969).

29. Fabos, *Model for Landscape Resource Assessment*, p. 36.

30. R. E. Byrson, "All Other Factors Being Constant . . . Theories of Global Climatic Change," in *Man's Impact on Environment*, ed. T. R. Detwyler, (New York: McGraw-Hill, 1971), pp. 167-174.

31. P. A. Leighton, "Geographical Aspects of Air Pollution," in ibid., pp. 113-130; A. M. Woorhees and Assoc., and Ryckman, Edgerley, Tomlinson, and Assoc., "Reducing Air Pollution through Land Use and Public Facility Planning," in *Land Use and the Environment: An Anthology of Readings* (Washington, D.C.: Environmental Protection Agency Office of Air Programs, 1972).

32. U.S., Federal Council for Science and Technology, Committee on Environmental Quality, "Noise—Sound without Value," in Detwyler, *Man's Impact on Environment*, pp. 175-189.

33. Boyce, Day, and McDonald, *Metropolitan Plan Making*, pp. 198-199.

34. J. Gy. Fabos and S. J. Caswell, *Composite Landscape Assessment*, Research Bulletin no. 637, University of Massachusetts, Agricultural Experiment Station, Amherst, Massachusetts, 1977, pp. 208-223.

35. J. Gy. Fabos, C. Greene, and S. A. Joyner, *The METLAND Landscape Planning Process*, Research Bulletin, University of Massachusetts, Agricultural Experiment Station, Amherst, Massachusetts (forthcoming).

36. Ibid., Chapter 5.

SUGGESTED READINGS

Burton, I. and Kates, R. W. *Readings in Resource Management and Conservation*. Chicago: University of Chicago Press, 1965.

Clawson, M. *Suburban Land Conversion in the United States: An Economic and Governmental Process*. Baltimore: Johns Hopkins Press for Resources for the Future, 1971.

Davis, K., ed. *Cities: Their Origin, Growth and Human Impact*. San

Francisco: W. H. Freeman and Co., 1973.
Detwyler, T. R., ed. *Man's Impact on the Environment.* New York: McGraw-Hill, 1971.
Detwyler, T. R., and Marcus, M. G. *Urbanization and Environment: The Physical Geography of the City.* Belmont, Calif.: Duxbury Press, 1972.
Gottman, J. *Megalopolis: The Urbanized Northeastern Seaboard of the United States.* Cambridge, Mass.: MIT Press, 1961.
Hoskins, W. G. *The Making of the English Landscape.* Baltimore: Penguin Books, 1955.
McHarg, I. *Design with Nature.* Garden City, N.Y.: Natural History Press, 1969.
Man's Impact on the Global Environment: Assessment and Recommendations for Action, Report of the Study of Critical Environmental Problems (SCEP). Sponsored by the Massachusetts Institute of Technology. Cambridge, Mass.: MIT Press, 1970.
Thomas, W. L., Jr. *Man's Role in Changing the Face of the Earth.* 2 vols. Chicago: University of Chicago Press, 1972.
Whyte, W. H. *The Last Landscape.* New York: Doubleday, 1970.

3 THE EVOLUTION OF LANDSCAPE PLANNING PRINCIPLES

The refinement of landscape planning principles is a relatively recent phenomenon. In other areas of planning, such as economics and transportation, a longer history of empirical inquiry resulted in a body of theory well developed by the 1950s. Only in the last twenty years has a concentrated examination of the causes and effects of environmental change brought about a comparable sophistication in the principles of land-based planning.

The interest in environmentally sensitive land use planning owes much of its current momentum to the research efforts of environmental scientists. In addition, there has been an enormous improvement in the technical tools available to land use planners. Computers and satellite imagery, for instance, have greatly facilitated the development of more realistic and reliable landscape planning principles. These advances in knowledge are extremely significant and will be discussed in detail in Chapter 4. However, the contribution of "knowledge" to refined planning principles should not obscure the role of "sensibility." That is, the facts should not only be known but also evaluated. For example, a community may know that some land is, for one reason or another, inappropriate for housing. However, unless their sensibilities lead them to be concerned about that impropriety, they are likely to ignore it. The continued residential expansion directly over California's San Andreas fault is a good example: people know that their actions may be imprudent, but their values, their sensibilities, lead them to discount the risk in favor of enjoying the benefits.

The development of environmental values—that way of looking at things that pays attention to environmental opportunities and limitations—is thus equally important to the development of landscape planning principles. Unlike empirical knowledge about the environment, however, these values have a long lineage, stretching back in western European thought at least to eighteenth-century romanticism. The history of this evolution of environmental values is important to an understanding of the current development of landscape planning. Before proposing four principles for contemporary landscape planning, therefore, the philosophical development of these principles will be outlined. It is hoped that this historical survey will illustrate not only the growth of these ideas but also the tradition in our society that they represent.

THE UTOPIANS

One branch of the landscape planning legacy can be traced to the reforming visions of utopian idealists. The proposals of thinkers such as Robert Owen, Le Corbusier, and Paolo Soleri, although dissimilar in many particulars, share the fundamental perception that a rationally planned community would resolve some of the problems of traditional urban development.

Owen was one of the first utopians to attempt to implement his vision. A Scottish mill owner who criticized the impact of contemporary industrial society on the lives of workers, he found a sizable following on both sides of the Atlantic in the early nineteenth century. He proposed the establishment of small communities whose initial economic basis would be agricultural, to be followed by manufacturing as the community coalesced.

Buildings were to be "planned square, with communal arrangements for domestic chores."[1] Although a few Owenite communities were actually begun, such as New Harmony, Indiana, each of them proved to be impractical and failed. Simple and somewhat paternalistic, Owen's ideas suffered from a misunderstanding of human behavior and from too little concern for the availability of industrial resources.

The "garden cities" proposed by Ebenezer Howard, an English inventor in the 1890s, were similarly motivated by a desire to overcome the problems of industrialized cities. Howard envisioned the creation of small communities of 30,000 people each. They would be located in the countryside, separated from existing urban areas by a "greenbelt" of permanently rural land.[2] Homes would be laid out on a circular pattern of streets. A few garden cities were built in England—Letchworth and Welwyn are the two principle examples—although in the space of fifty years they have become satellite suburbs of London rather than self-contained cities in their own right.

Other turn-of-the-century utopian town plans include the Ciudad Lineal ("lineal city") proposed by Arturo Soria y Mata for greater Madrid (1882) and the elaborate Cite Industrielle of Tony Garnier (1901). Although less motivated by a desire to escape from industrialization than those of Owen and Howards, both of these schemes dealt with only a portion of the problems of industrialized urban conditions.[3]

The utopian consciousness was not confined to the nineteenth century. Of the more modern proponents of ideal cities, two are singled out by Constantin Doxiadis, the Greek urbanist and planner, as the only "people [who] tried to face the problem [urbanization] as an entity."[4] The first was Le Corbusier, whose proposals in *La Ville Radieuse* (1925) and in *L'Urbanisme des Trois Etablissements Humains* (1959) called for the building of high-density cities characterized by huge high-rise structures. The second visionary cited by Doxiadis was the American architect Frank Lloyd Wright. In 1937 Wright first proposed his plan for a model city called "Broadacres" and recommended that each family in the community should live on at least one acre of their own land.

Probably the best known contemporary utopian is Paolo Soleri. From his compound in the American Southwest, Soleri has published plans for "objects of immense size that can support as many as a million people per cubic mile."[5] These gigantic "mega structures" are meant to rescue the ecology of the earth from the ravages of "horizontal sprawl." However, Soleri's vision, aside from its sociological and political implications, would seem to falter from its failure to address the issue of waste, certainly one of the major contributors to today's ecological stress.

Of course, Soleri's utopia is far from unique in its apparent impracticality and its logical lacunae. All of the proposals outlined above, for instance, failed to reckon with the decentralizing momentum of the twentieth century, with the single exception of Wright's Broadacres. Yet even Wright took little cognizance of the inherent qualities of the land in his vision of a homogeneous landscape pattern. Broadacres was to stretch in all directions, to be at once, "everywhere and nowhere." From the environmental standpoint, then, both the nineteenth-century and twentieth-century utopian solutions are culturally inadequate. Nonetheless, in their explicit concern for improving the quality of urban existence, they have contributed significantly to the evolution of progressive environmental values.

THE LANDSCAPE ARCHITECTS

The second major stream, perhaps the mainstream, of environmentally sensitive ideas has been occupied for over one hundred years by people who have called themselves landscape architects. The most important is the man often called the "father of American landscape architecture"—Frederick Law Olmsted, Sr. Most remembered for his role in the creation of Central Park in New York City, Olmsted was a remarkably perceptive planner as well. His ideas about the proper use of the landscape, though somewhat naive in the light of today's improved understanding of ecological processes, are nonetheless one of the earliest cogent expressions of environmental values. In his writings about the evils of haphazard urban growth—his term is "spread city"—Olmsted called not only for a healthy urban environment, but for a protected countryside as well.[6] Much of his perceptive understanding of the importance of rural resources developed during his early career as a "scientific farmer" on Staten Island during the years 1844 to 1854.[7]

Without the benefit of an extensive body of empirical ecological findings, Olmsted conceptualized the structure of industrial cities and suburban communities by drawing on his intuition and his observations of nature and society. His proposals for the community of Riverside near Chicago, presented in 1869, and for the Boston metropolitan park system in 1878 typically illustrate his appreciation of environmental issues.[8] The plans for Riverside dedicated the land along a river for use as a public park. He did not consult hydrologic data on the frequency of floods—they did not exist. Yet he understood that rivers periodically overflow and that it would be prudent to avoid unnecessary construction of houses or shops in the flood-prone area. Of course, there was the additional benefit that by placing the riverfront in the public ownership, its inherent aesthetic and recreational value could be enjoyed by the whole community.

Olmsted's plans for the first phase of the new park system for metropolitan Boston expanded the concept of riverfront parks to include the notion of linking the larger elements of a regional park network. Three towns, which at that time were suburbs of Boston—Roxbury, Dorchester, and Brookline—were connected by the Fenway, a streamfront park.[9]

Olmsted's proposals are significant in the evolution of landscape planning principles because they represent a radical change in attitude toward the natural environment within urban areas. His plans exhibited a desire to work in harmony with nature, which contrasted markedly with the prevailing thought, which saw economic and political objectives (and occasionally social objectives) as the principle concerns of urban development. Olmsted always assessed the land and its capabilities before formulating a plan for its development. Although his assessment techniques were not sophisticated, his intention was thoroughly modern. This philosophical consanguinity Olmsted shares with today's landscape planners is perhaps nowhere more evident than in the title of Ian McHarg's famous book on ecologically sensitive planning—*Design with Nature* (1969).

The planners of today have access to an arsenal of scientific information and technical means that would have left Olmsted amazed and excited. The description of some of these developments is the focus of this book. It is important for us to realize, however, that the explosion in the technology of landscape assessment, although in many ways a contemporary phenomenon, also has its roots in the romantic and progressive movements of the nineteenth century.

There is a venerable tradition of scientific observation in our history, reaching back through such remarkable Renaissance observers as da Vinci, at least to Francis of Assisi. One of the significant nineteenth-century innovations in this field was the attention paid to the *interaction* between natural phenomena and human activities. A seminal volume, *Man and Nature,* was published by George Perkins Marsh in 1865.[10] In this book, Marsh, who was a philologist, undertook to summarize the scientific understanding of human impact on the envrionment as it existed in his time. Most importantly for the evolution of landscape planning principles, Marsh for the first time raised questions about the "uncertainties" resulting from the expanding use of the natural environment by industrialized society—or as Leo Marx said, from the introduction of "the machine into the garden."

The response of landscape architects to the increase in environmental awareness stimulated by Marsh and his colleagues is illustrated by Charles Eliot's expansion of Olmsted's Boston metropolitan park network. A protege of Olmsted, Eliot was impressed by the success of park planning in London and Paris and became determined to create a comparable public open space framework for the burgeoning Boston metropolis.[11] By 1890, the city of Boston had annexed towns lying ten miles from its center, in areas served by the radial railroad and streetcar lines. Eliot appreciated this link between new urban development and routes of the street railways.[12] He proposed (and helped to implement) a regional development plan that allotted land along the trolleys to high-density uses but that created an extensive park system in the interstices (Figure 12). This park system was designed, in Eliot's words, to place into public use the "spaces on the ocean front, much of the shores and islands of [Boston] Bay, the courses of the large areas of wild forest on the outer rim [of the metropolitan region] and numerous small squares, playgrounds, and parks in the midst of the dense population."[13]

An analysis of Eliot's plans reveals their importance in the development of landscape planning. The metropolitan park scheme exhibited an understanding of areas of special resource value as well as those hazardous to health. The plans also reveal Eliot's awareness not only of the importance, but also of the fragility of important natural systems such as estuaries and beaches. He urged the protection of an entire river basin as a watershed to supply the future water needs of the metropolis.[14] "A considerable tract of land," he wrote, "should be taken for the purpose of guarding the water supply against pollution. It should be kept in as natural a condition as possible, for the most part covered with a varied forest-growth, and include a storage basin of a lake-like character."[15] His understanding of how overuse affected the ecology of beaches led him to recommend specific devices to redeem abused areas.[16]

Eliot also implicitly knew that some areas of the landscape had qualities well suited for development. When selecting the site for a college or, more traditionally, a parkway, he analyzed the available maps of the United States Geologic Survey for topography, vegetation, and streams.[17] His use of these maps, with their roads depicted in "black, streams in blue, and twenty-feet

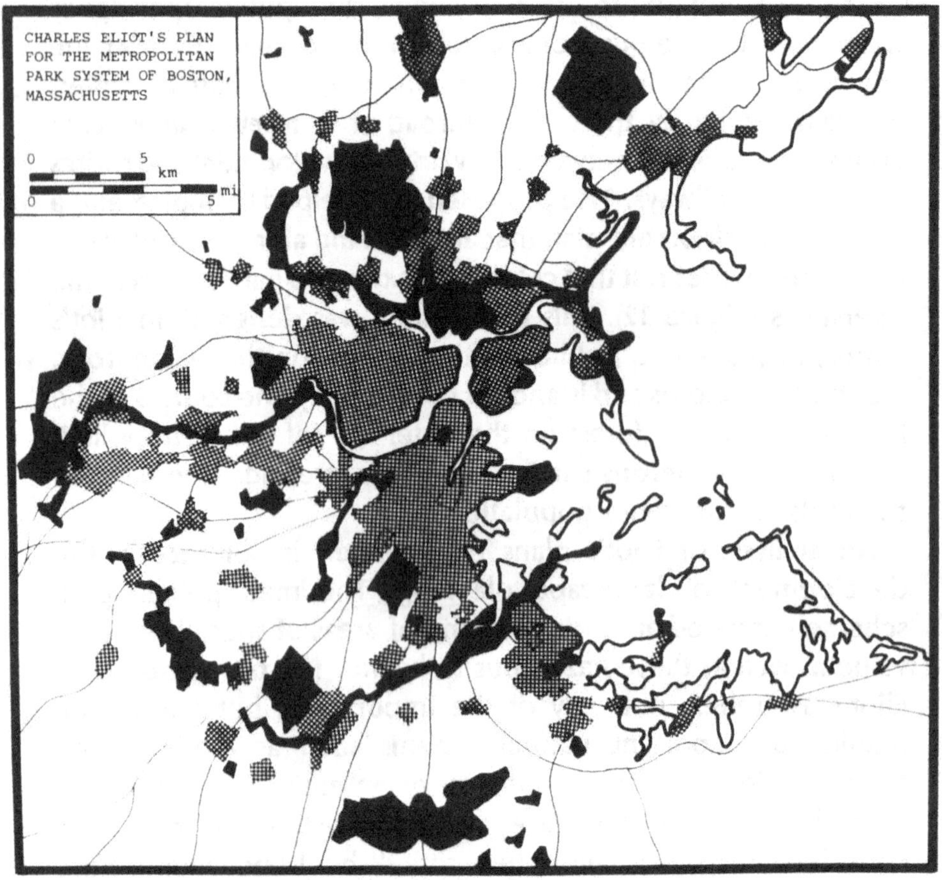

FIGURE 12. Charles Eliot's plan for the Boston metropolis provided the open space framework for about a 250-square-mile area at the turn of the century. This plan represents one of the earlier attempts at landscape planning. (Dark areas represent public open spaces.)

contours in red,"[18] is significant in its own right for it illustrates a recognition of the value of finding and using available data, even if they have been collected for purposes other than planning.

In short, in his practice of planning in accordance with the "law of nature" and in his advocacy of "the adaptation of environment and purpose, in the playing out of whatever work may need to be done,"[19] Charles Eliot was the apotheosis of the nineteenth-century landscape architect; his role in the evolution of landscape planning principles cannot be challenged.

THE "SCIENTIST-PLANNERS"

The twentieth-century advances in landscape planning principles are as significant as those of Olmsted's time. Many advances have been stimulated by empirical research findings in the environmental sciences. Geology, pedology, hydrology, climatology, and ecology—all have contributed greatly to the human understanding of how the environment functions. Interestingly, these sciences have also produced some of the most important theorists in landscape planning.

Sir Patrick Geddes (1854-1932) was a Scottish biologist and sociologist. Alerted by his scientific training to the issues of interaction between human beings and their natural surroundings, Geddes pioneered many efforts aimed at resolving environmental conflict. Among his many contributions were the development of refined landscape survey techniques and the proposal of a classification system of natural resources. He conceived numerous interpretive exhibits for museums and exhibitions, exhibits that anticipated today's multimedia environmental education efforts by fifty years. His theory of planning, worked out over many years, was based on "geotechnics"—a means of restoring the earth and its resources through modern scientific methods.[20]

Geddes had a trans-Atlantic counterpart in the American forester, Benton MacKaye. Working around Boston, like Olmsted and Eliot before him, MacKaye worked out one of the earliest "ecosytem" approaches to the planning of a modern metropolitan region (Figure 13). Based on a careful analysis of the entire landscape, he identified several categories of land that were especially valuable or fragile and as such should be protected from development. These areas, which included topograhic ridges, steep slopes, canyons, river floodplains, swamps, lakes, and shorelines, would act, MacKaye argued, as natural "levees," controlling the "metropolitan invasion."[21] Eliot's earlier plan for Boston had been intended to accommodate the sort of linear growth generated by expanding rail transportation. MacKaye's

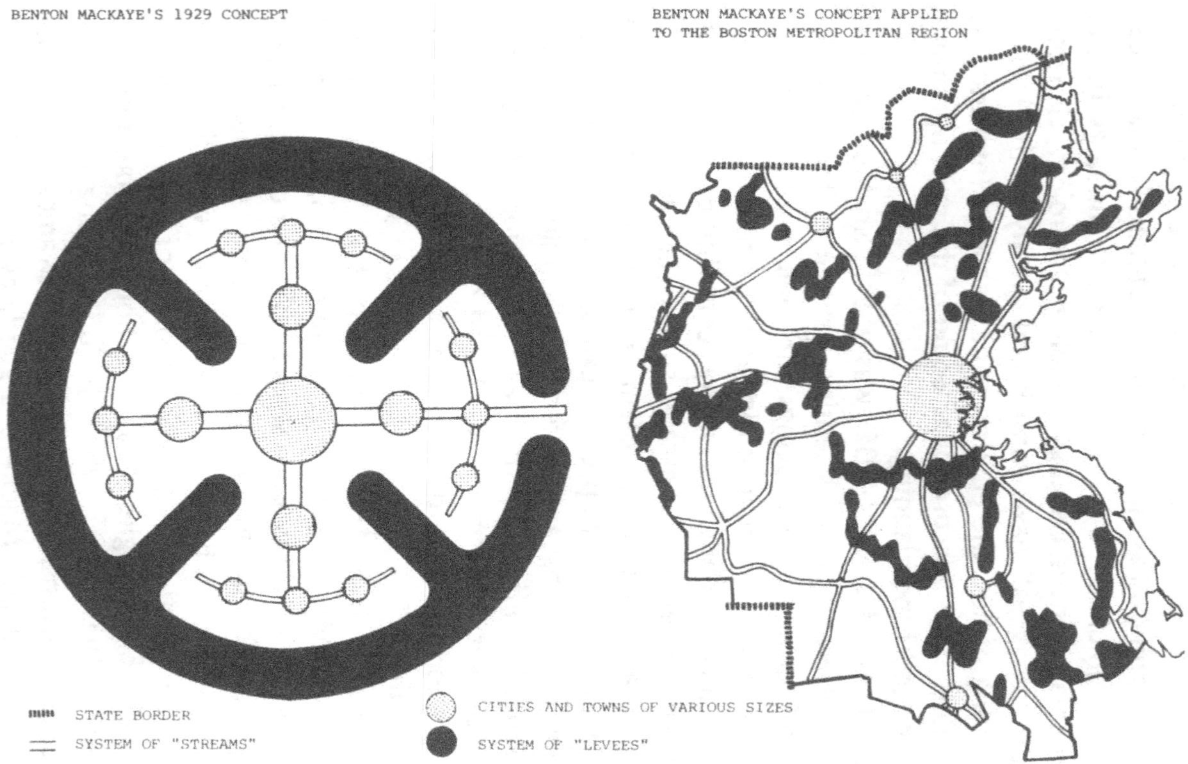

FIGURE 13. Benton MacKaye's regional approach (1929) to the problem of open space and urban encroachment. MacKaye believed that what he described as "systems of levees," such as natural wetland systems, could control the metropolitan "invasion" ("flow").

proposals, published in 1928 under the title *The New Exploration,* represent the first attempt to deal with the extraordinary decentralizing pressures of urban expansion in the age of the automobile.

In recent years, many of the most prominent scientists-turned-planners have had their early training in ecology. In Great Britain, the lessons of ecology for land use planning have been ably articulated in the works of Darling[22] and Dasmann, Milton, and Freeman.[23] In the United States, perhaps the foremost theorist of ecologically based planning has been Eugene Odum. A respected academic ecologist and author of one of the major college texts on the subject,[24] Odum has formulated an elegant model of land use allocation based on ecological principles.[25] This model classifies all land into one of four "compartments" depending on its function in the regional ecosystem. These compartments are: (1) *protective* zones, where natural systems function relatively undisturbed by human activity and thus should be "protected"; (2) *productive* zones, where natural systems are modified by human beings in order to increase their production of food or fiber for human use; (3) *nonvital* zones, where urban development has totally supplanted natural ecologic function and, finally; (4) *compromise* zones, which are characterized by a combination of any of the above compartments; these Odum calls multiuse zones. The significance of Odum's formulation stems from its consideration of human activity as a factor in the ecosystem analysis. By objectively describing the full environmental continuum rather than only the "natural" areas, it can facilitate realistic ecological consideration of land development decisions.

LANDSCAPE PLANNING PRINCIPLES: SOME CURRENT PROPOSALS

The interrelated issues of improved urban development and the impact of humans on the environment were raised, as we have seen, by the middle of the nineteenth century. In the past one hundred years, the combined efforts of both scientists and visionaries have provided us with some of the understanding and sensibility needed to address these issues adequately. There is a rich literature describing the environment and human actions and attitudes toward it—e.g., T. R. Detwyler's *Man's Impact on the Environment.*[26] Naivete about the function of the natural environment can no longer be used as an excuse for not dealing with these effects. The inchoate concepts of Marsh and Olmsted can and should be coalesced into a set of guiding principles for our future use of the landscape. The four principles outlined below are proposed to meet this need and, in particular, to aid in the making of decisions about urban expansion within the metropolis.

1. *Development should be discouraged in areas of significant resource value.* Many of the requirements and amenities of modern urban life—ranging from food to attractive scenery to gravel for concrete construction—are currently available only outside our urbanized areas. Much of this local scarcity can be avoided by identifying the location of these biological, physical, and aesthetic resources within the region and by acting to prevent their needless degradation or obliteration. This is not a call for metropolitan regions to be entirely self-sufficient. Rather, it is a response to the growing realization that many of the commodities either currently imported into metropolitan areas at great expense in money and energy (such as drinking water and gravel) or simply unavailable in metropolitan areas (such as scenic views) *would have been* locally available if haphazard, unplanned development had not obliterated, degraded, or made inaccessible the local supply.

2. *Development should be discouraged in areas of natural and man-made hazard.* The losses and hardship that result from such natural hazards as floods and such human-caused hazards as noise and air pollution accrue not only to the people and properties immediately affected, but also to the wider society that is called on to provide relief to the victims. Much of the impact of hazards can be avoided, especially when areas of high risk can be identified in advance.

3. *Development should be encouraged in the areas best suited for it.* The costs associated with developing land for typical urban uses often increase owing to unfavorable site conditions, such as slope. The costs of living on a site, once developed, can also increase owing to the nature of the site. It costs more and uses more energy, for instance, to heat a house in New England when it is located on a north-facing slope, exposed to winter winds and receiving little sun, rather than on a protected southern slope. Third, the amenity associated with any development can depend on its site as well. Thus, although it is highly unlikely that any land will exhibit excellent suitability from all points of view, it is clear that unnecessary cost and loss of amenity can be minimized if the landscape is analyzed for its development suitability and if development activities are directed to the best areas.

4. *The ecological "carrying capacity" of the regional environment should not be exceeded.* Odum's "compartmental" model of ecosystem development implies that it is possible to determine the sort and amount of devlopment that is conducive to maintain an optimal degree of ecological stability and productivity. If a value is to be put on minimizing the unnecessary degradation of the environment, then its "carrying capacity"—its ability to accommodate human activities without being irreparably damaged—must be identified and respected.

Several comments about these principles are in order. First, it is important to realize that they occasionally can (and will when applied) be mutually contradictory. The land most suitable for development, for instance, may also be regularly flooded and a significant source of groundwater for drinking. However, this is not a liability. In fact, if these issues are raised to the level of conscious assessment, it should be easier to make informed decisions about the trade-off between conflicting goals. An example of a specific process to resolve these conflicts is proposed in Part 3 (Chapter 9).

Second, and most important in the context of this book, the implementation of these landscape planning principles depends on the ability to assess easily and accurately the quantity, quality, location, and distribution of each of the landscape characteristics covered by the principles. To this end, the state of the art of quantitative assessment for resources, hazards, development suitability, and ecological impact is outlined in Part 2 (Chapters 5-8).

Finally, the ultimate significance of these four principles, as with any, lies in their implementation. For them to become operable some basic and systemic changes must occur in the ways that decisions about land use are made. These changes are essentially political, and a detailed discussion of how to make them is beyond the scope of this text. However, there are several instances in the history of social change when the mere availability of resource data or the result of landscape assessment has effected change. Such information can act as a catalyst in resolving the political consequences. It is hoped that the techniques and ideas discussed here will help to bring about this kind of catalysis.

NOTES

1. J. F. C. Harrison, *Robert Owen and the Owenites in Britain and America* (London: Routledge and Kegan Paul, 1969), p. 29.
2. E. Howard, *Garden Cities of To-morrow* (London: Faber and Faber; Cambridge, Mass.: MIT Press, 1965).
3. C. A. Doxiadis, *Between Dystopia and Utopia* (Hartford, Conn.: Trinity College Press, 1966), p. 34.
4. Ibid.
5. P. Soleri, *Visionary Cities: The Arcology of Paolo Soleri* (New York: Praeger, 1971).
6. A. Fein, *Frederick Law Olmsted and the American Environmental Tradition* (New York: Braziller, 1972), p. 33.
7. Ibid., p. 163.
8. J. Gy. Fabos, G. T. Milde, and V. M. Weinmayr, *Frederick Law Olmsted, Sr.: Founder of Landscape Architecture in America* (Amherst, Mass.: University of Massachusetts Press, 1968), pp. 47-74.
9. Ibid.
10. G. P. Marsh, *Man and Nature* (1865; reprint ed., Cambridge, Mass.: The Belknap Press of Harvard University Press, 1965).

11. C. W. Eliot, *Charles Eliot: Landscape Architect* (Boston: Houghton Mifflin, 1902).
12. Ibid., p. 511.
13. Ibid., p. 381.
14. Ibid., p. 351.
15. Ibid., p. 19.
16. Ibid., p. 347.
17. Ibid., pp. 297-537.
18. Ibid., p. 297.
19. Ibid., p. 663.
20. M. Stalley, *Patrick Geddes: Spokesman for Man and the Environment* (New Brunswick, N.J.: Rutgers University Press, 1972), pp. 15, 27, 33, and 264.
21. Benton MacKaye, *The New Exploration: A Philosophy of Regional Planning* (1928; reprinted., Urbana: University of Illinois Press, 1962), pp. 168-200.
22. F. F. Darling, *Wilderness and Plenty* (Boston: Houghton Mifflin, 1970).
23. R. F. Dasmann, J. P. Milton, and P. H. Freeman, *Ecological Principles for Economic Development* (New York: John Wiley and Sons, 1973).
24. E. P. Odum, *Fundamentals of Ecology,* 3rd ed. (Philadelphia: Saunders, 1971).
25. E. P. Odum, "The Strategy of Eco-system Development," *Science* 164 (April 1969):262-270.
26. T. R. Detwyler, ed., *Man's Impact on the Environment* (New York: McGraw-Hill, 1971).

SUGGESTED READINGS

Dassman, R. F. *Environmental Conservation.* New York: John Wiley and Sons, 1968.

Eliot, C. W. *Charles Eliot: Landscape Architect.* Boston: Houghton Mifflin, 1902.

Fabos, J. Gy.; Milde, G. T.; and Weinmayr, V. M. *Frederick Law Olmsted, Sr., Founder of Landscape Architecture in America.* Amherst, Mass.: University of Massachusetts Press, 1968.

Fein, A. *Frederick Law Olmsted and the American Environmental Tradition.* New York: Braziller, 1972.

——. *Landscape into City Scape; Frederick Law Olmsted's Plans for a*

Greater New York City. Ithaca, N.Y.: Cornell University Press, 1968.

Howard, E. *Garden Cities of To-morrow*. Cambridge, Mass.: MIT Press, 1965.

MacKaye, Benton. *The New Exploration: A Philosophy of Regional Planning*. Urbana: University of Illinois Pres, 1962.

Marsh, G. P. *Man and Nature*. Edited by David Lowenthal. Cambridge, Mass.:Belknap Press of Harvard University Press, 1965.

Mumford, L. *The Story of Utopias*. New York: Viking Press, 1962.

Nash, R. *Wilderness and the American Mind*. New Haven: Yale University Press, 1967.

Odum, E. *Ecology*. New York: Holt, Rinehart and Winston, 1963.

Stalley, M., ed. *Sir Patrick Geddes: Spokesman for Man and the Environment*. New Brunswick, N.J.: Rutgers University Press, 1972.

Stein, C. S. *Towards New Towns for America*. Cambridge, Mass.: MIT Press, 1951.

4 THE TOOLS OF LANDSCAPE PLANNING

One of the major concepts underlying the several landscape planning principles outlined in the last chapter is that decisions on the use of land should always be preceded by an assessment of its inherent characteristics. This chapter considers some of the practical tools of landscape assessment currently available to planners. For the purposes of discussion, these tools are divided into four groups. The first—remote sensing—deals with the collection of information about the landscape. The second and third—statistical analysis and computerized data manipulation—include the primary tools for analyzing the information gathered through remote sensing. Finally, the fourth group—systems analysis and modeling—describes methods of pulling together the analyzed information in a way that clarifies the landscape implications of land use policy decisions. This process is often referred to as "synthesis."

REMOTE SENSING

The term *remote sensing* is a relatively recent addition to the jargon of geographers and planners, although the activity it describes has been around for over fifty years. This activity is the gathering of information about the surface of the earth with the aid of cameras or cameralike devices mounted on airplanes (or, in more recent times, satellites). The technology of remote sensing has expanded greatly in the years since World War II, enabling the mapping of a remarkable range of attributes of the physical landscape. However, before describing the present-day capabilities of remote sensing, it may be useful to recapitulate some of the developments in mapmaking that have prepared the way for the current levels of sophistication.

The quest for more accurate representation of geographic information has existed for centuries. Some of the earliest efforts in this area were developed as aids to oceanic navigation. By the height of the Renaissance, however, the most advanced cartographic techniques had yielded but relatively simple and crude charts. The famous *portolano* folio of 1500, for instance, identified only the general location of major ports and delineated selected sailing directions by means of rhumb lines. The atlas of G. M. Mercator, published in 1594, marked a significant advance, although even these maps showed rough and inaccurate continental outlines.

The Industrial Revolution brought several significant developments in the mapping of land surfaces. In the United States, the survey and mapping technology of the late eighteenth century established the basic pattern of land development and resource exploitation for the entire area west of the Appalachian Mountains. In 1785, Congress established a rectilinear system of ordinance survey, which resulted in the mapping of a grid of six-mile-square "township" boundaries across the entire country. This technique, made possible by the ability to lay out straight lines in a north to south or east to west direction, proved to be a significant catalyst to the redistribution of land from the native Americans to the pioneering settlers. At the same time, however, it imposed rigid boundaries, which often did not fit topographic and other natural boundaries.[1] It was a "square survey for a rounded countryside."

Before 1800, the making of maps showing land areas had

concentrated on the depiction of political and ownership boundaries and travel routes. The nineteenth-century exploitation of the American West, however, stimulated the beginning of geologic and topographic mapping. The early topographic maps were limited to a few selected regions, but the ones that were available were especially useful in the selection of railroad rights-of-way.[2] The importance of these mapping activities was formalized in 1879, when the United States Geological Survey was established to take the responsibility for all official geologic and topographic cartography.[3]

One of the biggest challenges of mapmaking before the twentieth century was the graphic representation of an area of land as if seen from above while using data collected on the ground. With the invention of the airplane, the recording of land as it actually looks from the air finally became feasible. The potential of airplanes for this task was recognized by none other than Wilbur Wright, who took the first recorded aerial photograph from a plane in 1909. The technique of aerial photogrammetry—the making of maps based on measurements taken from aerial photographs—was refined greatly during World War I, and by 1922, the U.S. Geological Survey had produced its first quadrangle map using aerial photographs.

Today, conventional aerial photography is still the most commonly used form of remote sensing. Up-to-date, black-and-white (panchromatic) photos are available for virtually any inhabited region in the country. Most of these photos are available in stereoscopic pairs, in which the same area on the ground is photographed from two angles. When viewed through a stereoscope, these overlapping pictures create an illusion of three-dimensionality, so that buildings, vegetation, and landforms have an almost tangible reality.

The transference of information interpreted from aerial photographs onto maps can take place at many scales and for many purposes. Aerial photography is most often used by planners as a source of land use data. Several systematic photo-interpretation procedures have been developed for this purpose. Most are based on a taxonomic classification of general categories and detailed types of surface cover. A classification used in the mapping of the state of Massachusetts, for instance, includes six categories of land cover: agricultural, forest, wetland, mining, outdoor recreation, and urban. Each of these categories is further divided into more than a hundred different "surface cover types," such as tilled land, unused tilled land, pasture, abandoned pasture, and orchards.[4]

The potential utility of detailed, systematic land use (surface cover) mapping for planners is great. The Massachusetts classification system described above was used to produce detailed interpretative maps for the entire state in 1952. The entire process was repeated in 1971, using the same classification but using photographs taken nearly twenty years later. A comparison of maps for the two points in time not only documented the development that had occurred during the period but also indicated the many secondary land use changes that had occurred, such as the decline in actively farmed land. Figure 14 shows an example of a panchromatic photograph used in Massachusetts survey together with the surface cover map interpreted from the photo.

Conventional aerial photography is also used to prepare soil and surficial geology maps. In these applications, it is frequently necessary to corroborate the interpretation of the photographs with numerous on-site investigations.

Although it is still the most widespread remote sensing technology, conventional aerial photography has several inherent limitations. The most obvious is that photos of the ground can be obtained only on cloud-free days. The preparation of controlled and accurate maps from photographs is time-consuming and expensive because the interpretation is done by people. Most important, perhaps, panchromatic photographs are sensitive only to visible light, whose wavelength ranges from 0.4 to 0.7 microns (Figure 15). This is a very small window on the electromagnetic spectrum. One of the consequences of this limitation is that it is often difficult to differentiate objects that exhibit similar shades of gray. Several techniques have been developed to overcome some

FIGURE 14. A conventional airphoto and a typical detailed land use distribution map in Massachusetts as interpreted from airphotos with the aid of a stereoscope. (Land uses are keyed by letter abbreviations. For example, HW for highway as shown on the left side, or UR for a low-density urban residential use in the top right corner.)

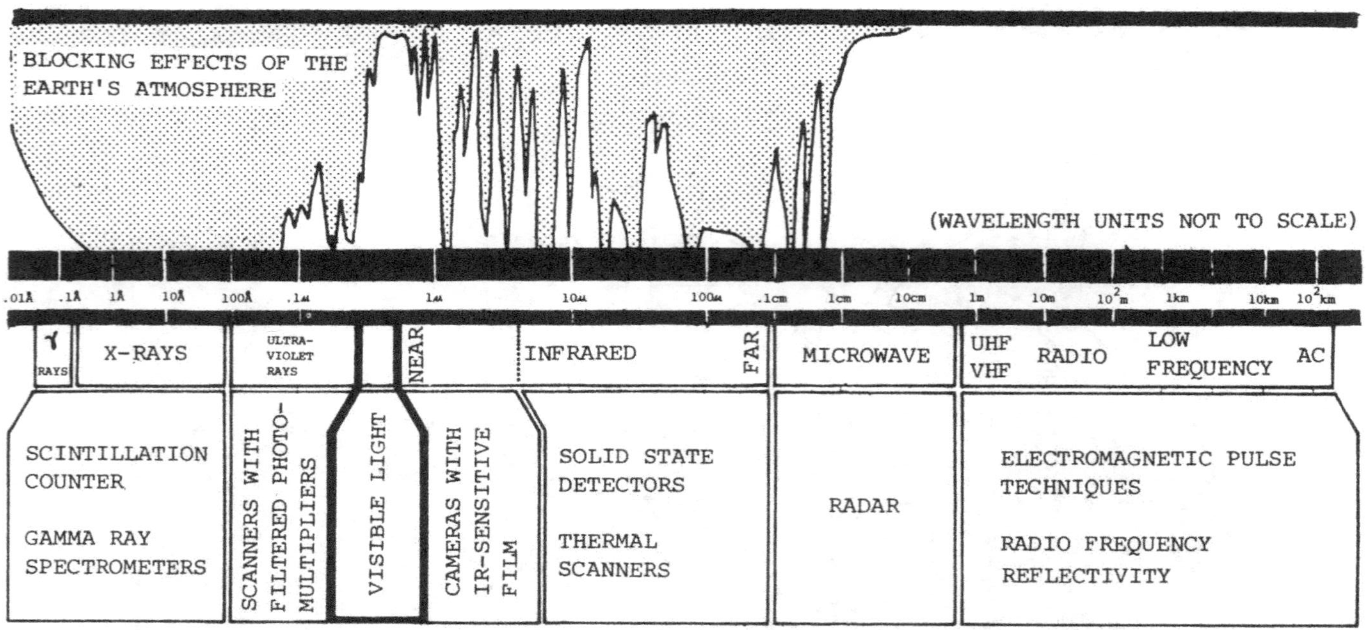

FIGURE 15. The electromagnetic spectrum. Various remote sensing techniques are listed in the bottom section. Note the tiny segment visible to man.

of the limitations of conventional photography. By using film sensitive to additional segments of the spectrum, such as the "near" infra-red (0.7 to 7.0 micron wavelength), for instance, or filters that selectively "edit" the range of wavelengths that reach the film, additional characteristics of the recorded images can be discerned. A recently developed device consists of a number of camera units, each with a different combination of film and filter, which can provide up to nine separate images of the same area of ground. The procedure of "multiband reconnaissance," as it is known, also extends into the ultraviolet range of the electromagnetic spectrum. The special characteristics of ultraviolet radiation give heightened contrast to certain landscape elements, such as unpainted metal roofs and limestone outcrops, thereby increasing their distinguishability.

Two other remote techniques also extend the range of electromagnetic sensing considerably.[5] The first is the detection of heat by specially designed scanners. This "thermal" sensing circumvents many of the temporal or atmospheric conditions that impeded most other remote sensors. Thermal surveillance can be carried out at night as well as during the day, and the images taken through clouds, haze, or smoke are as detailed as those taken on a clear day. Thermal images are not, however, photographs in the usual sense. A thermal scanner detects variations in heat-radiating objects, variations that are then electronically amplified and either recorded on magnetic tape or projected on a cathode ray tube similar to a television.

Radar technology has also been developed for remote sensing. The principal technique is called "side-looking airborne radar," or SLAR. Radar, like thermal reconnaissance, can record images through all but the heaviest rain. The images it yields are also electronically transformed to make them visible and are usually produced in continuous strips rather than discrete photos (Figure 16).

Undoubtedly the most significant development in remote sensing in recent years is the use of devices mounted on orbiting satellites. In 1972, the first Earth Resources Technology Satellite

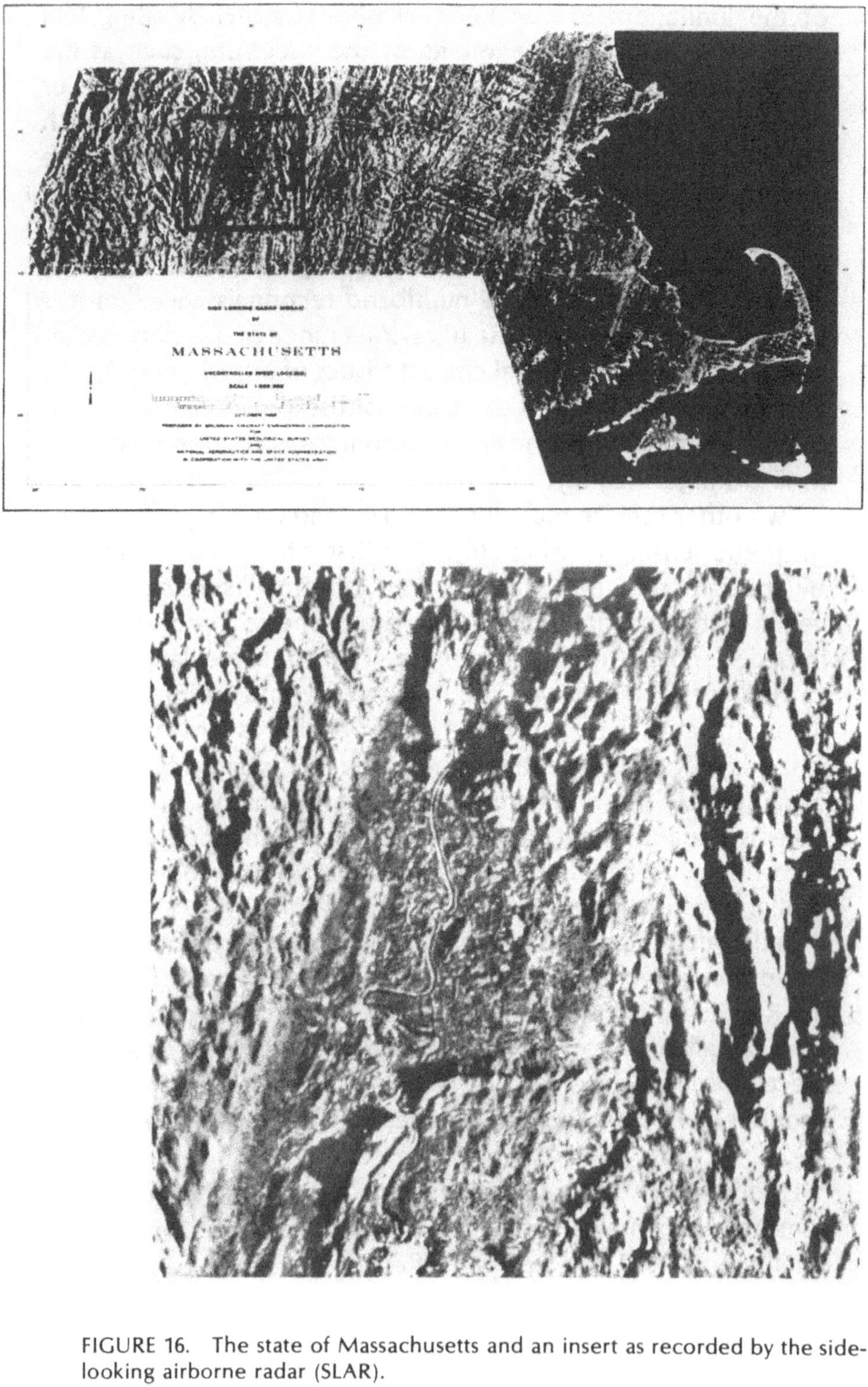

FIGURE 16. The state of Massachusetts and an insert as recorded by the side-looking airborne radar (SLAR).

(ERTS) was launched into a nonstationary orbit that brings it over every region of the earth on a fourteen-day cycle.[6] Fitted with highly sophisticated sensing equipment, ERTS records electromagnetic data from the earth's surface and beams them to receiving stations. There the data can be analyzed directly by computer or transformed into an actual visual image. Each image represents 10,000 square kilometers of ground. It is made up of 16 million individual cells for which one of 250 electromagnetic radiation values has been recorded. This is an extraordinary degree of detail: each cell corresponds to an area 25 meters square, or roughly one-sixth of an acre.

In summary, developments in remote sensing technology in the past two decades have placed an impressive amount of data at the disposal of land use planners. It has been estimated that some 90 percent of these data are not even utilized,[7] partly because of a lag in the development of comparably sophisticated techniques for analyzing and manipulating the information. A reasonable arsenal of analytical tools is available to planners, however, many of which have been developed in other fields. A brief survey of these methods follows.

STATISTICAL ANALYSIS

During the mid–nineteenth century, Gregor Mendel, an Austrian biologist, studied the ways in which pea plants differ from one another in height, in the color of their seeds, and in the color of their flowers. In the course of his experiments, he arrived at several conclusions, although he analyzed only a small sample of the entire population of pea plants. Mendel's methodology was one of earliest instances of statistical analysis, and from that point on, both the utility and capabilities of statistics for scientific investigation have expanded enormously. Of course, statistics have also shown a potential for misuse both by unwitting but well-meaning investigators and by all-too-witting propagandists and advertising copywriters.[8] It is imperative, therefore, to begin any discussion of statistical analysis for landscape planning with a clear understanding of what statistics are and what they can do. A good general definition is offered by Remington and Schork: "Statistics is a study of methods and procedures for collecting, classifying, summarizing, and analyzing data, and for making scientific inferences from such data."[9] As this definition implies, statistics can be used for two basic objectives: description and inference. Descriptive statistics are probably best known by the general public, for it is this form that is most often used by journalists, advertisers, and public opinion surveyors to organize and present numerical information.

Descriptive statistics have considerable utility in the assessment of landscape characteristics. In the analysis of vegetation, for instance, the statistical distribution of the types of trees and their heights and densities provides a concise indication of the character of a forest stand. This is a relatively simple example, but it should be noted that statistical description can also be considerably more complex.

The focus of much of modern statistics, however, is statistical inference, in which descriptive statistics are manipulated and analyzed to derive probabilistic conclusions from incomplete information. Inferential statistics can also be used to predict the mathematical likelihood of future events based on the characteristics of their past occurrence. In landscape assessment, these functions have many uses, ranging from the identification of land areas that are likely to be flooded to the estimation of the productivity of various soil types.

Nearly all of the statistical techniques mentioned so far must use numerical data. In the behavioral sciences, such numerical information is often not available. In this case, it may be appropriate to use "nonparametric" statistical techniques. Nonparametric statistics analyze elements that do not have a characteristic magnitude but that do have an ordinal (or ranked) relationship to one another.[10]

In landscape planning, nonparametric statistics are useful for two general areas of investigation. The first is in the assessment of landscape *quality*. It may be hypothesized, for instance, that most people prefer a predominantly natural environment to a predominantly human-made one, implying that environmental quality increases as "naturalness" increases. It might therefore be desirable to understand how people ascribe value to various degrees of "naturalness" in the landscape. For this task, the nonparametric "Q-sort" test can be used, in which respondents are provided with photographs of landscapes that exhibit varying degrees of naturalness. They are then asked to sort the photos into piles ranging from most to least preferred.

The "Q-sort" and many more complex techniques have been explored in recent years by several environmental psychologists.[11] Their research into human behavior and preference with respect to environmental quality has produced a growing body of findings, whose relevance and usefulness for landscape planning are becoming increasingly appreciated.[12]

The second area where landscape planners use nonparametric statistics is in the sampling of public attitudes toward various environmental resources, as an aid to generating alternative land use strategies. It may be useful to know, for instance, how the residents in a community value visual quality in comparison with agricultural productivity, forest productivity, and local groundwater. It may also be desirable to be able to compare the perceptions of the general public with those of local decision makers, developers, and environmentalists. A consensus among all groups that visual quality ranks higher than, say, local water supply could provide a planner with important guidance in preparing land use or management proposals.

In short, a great deal of the analysis of data in landscape planning is carried out with statistical tools. Descriptive statistics continue to be most widely utilized, but the use of statistics as a means of inferring and predicting is becoming more common. Finally, when the data are not amenable to numerical expression, various nonparametric devices provide a means to gain a detailed analysis.

COMPUTERIZED DATA STORAGE, RETRIEVAL, AND MANIPULATION

There are many techniques for storing and retrieving geographical information. A technique familiar to most people is the large roll-down map found in classrooms around the world. Here general information about a local province, for example, or the world as a whole, has been printed on oilcloth and rolled up or "stored" on a window shade-like device, ready to be "retrieved" at a moment's notice.

The introduction of computer technology to this relatively straightforward process has been necessitated by the enormous amount of geographical data now available. Even discounting the sixteen hundred bits of data per square kilometer that ERTS revises every fourteen days, the boon in environmental information is staggering. Consider Massachusetts, with an area of some 5,000,000 acres, the sixth smallest state in the United States. Data are readily available about the land use, soil type, and vegetation type, size, and density for each acre in the state. The storage of this information alone requires a capacity of two and one-half million bits of data.

Of course, the usefulness of this data depends not only on our ability to record and retrieve it easily. The assessment and analysis of many landscape parameters (such as forest productivity, flood hazard potential, and physical development suitability) often require that the relationships among several environmental variables be determined: there needs to be a convenient way of *manipulating* data.

The technology of geographic data manipulation as well as that of data storage and retrieval has been developing rapidly since the early 1960s. The outlines of three major innovations in the field are discussed below.

The "first generation" of data mapping and manipulating systems for computers is the *manually stored grid system,* as exemplified by the SYMAP program developed at Harvard University. In this technique, the user superimposes a rectilinear grid on a source map, such as the land use map shown in Figure 14 above. For each of the squares, or "cells," in the grid, the pertinent information from the underlying map is recorded, either on computer punch cards or magnetic tape. The information is then stored in the computer's memory bank as a matrix of individual cell ratings or designations. The computer can then be instructed to retrieve the data and to depict it by displaying or printing out a grid map shaded with up to ten tones of gray (Figure 17). In addition, the computer can be instructed to produce a composite grid map, which results from the overlay of two or more of its stored data matrices.[13]

The major feature of this system is the ability to calculate the combined effect of several factors using the overlay procedure. Its difficulties include a rather gross minimum size of grid cell (2.5 acres in most manual systems). Geographic data such as soil types and land uses are seldom rectilinear in configuration, and therefore the generalization of data to a large-scale grid results in a considerable loss of detail. The manual recording of grid cell values at the data preparation stage is also very time-consuming.

In the second generation of mapping and manipulation techniques, some of these deficiencies have been alleviated. *Computerized grid systems,* such as COMLUP, developed in the early 1970s, are identical to the manually recorded grid programs in basic concept.[14] However, the initial manual superimposition of a grid onto a base map and the reading off of cell values are replaced by a procedure in which the boundaries of irregular parcels on the base map are recorded automatically on a device known as a "digitizer." In the process of digitizing, the boundaries of all parcels are divided into a number of straight-line segments, and the Cartesian coordinates of the end points of each segment are recorded electronically. These points can be converted back into a two-dimensional map by using an automatic drafting machine, known as a "plotter."

The second innovation of COMLUP-like systems is that the division of the digitized base map into a grid of rectilinear cells is also carried out automatically and internally by the computer. In addition to saving time, the size of the cells in this type of program

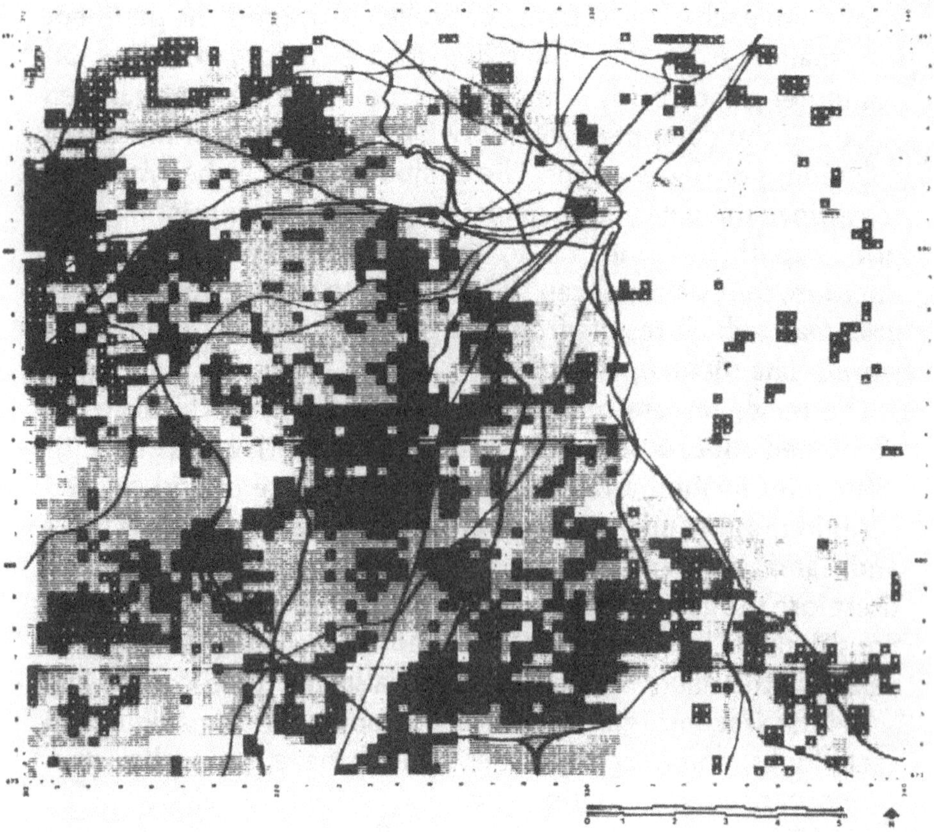

FIGURE 17. An application of manually stored grid system showing change in slope in the Boston region. (Darker tones denote steeper slopes.)

are much smaller than in the previously discussed systems. The cell size in COMLUP, for instance, is 0.2 acres. As shown in Figure 18, this results in a much more sensitive interpretation of the parcel boundaries of source data.

The third generation of technology in this field is only now beginning to develop. Several recent efforts, including research by the Canada Land Inventory group in Ottawa and by the Raytheon Corporation, have been aimed at developing an *area boundary system* of geographic data handling. In this procedure, a superimposed rectilinear grid is not required, and irregularly bounded maps can be overlaid directly. As of this writing, these

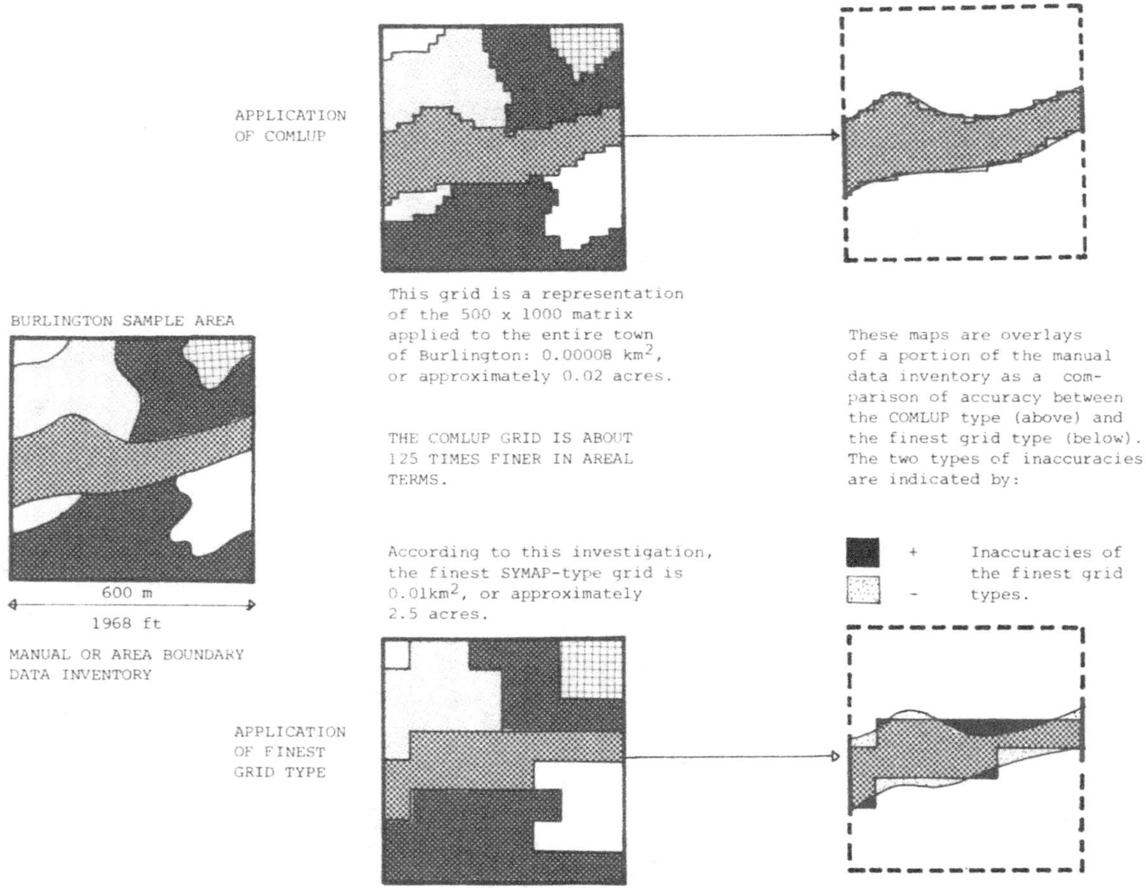

FIGURE 18. Comparison at a similar regional scale between the accuracy of the older, manually stored grid system of the 1960s and that of the computerized grid system developed during the early 1970s.

systems are still experimental, but they will probably be successfully applied to planning uses in the near future.

SYSTEMS ANALYSIS AND MODELING

The explosion in the amount of data and the sophistication of the analytic techniques that have recently become available to landscape planners point to the need for a comprehensive understanding of the interaction among numerous environmental factors and their function in the real world. In this task, the perspective of systems analysis and modeling—as explored by ecologists, geographers, environmental geologists, and hydrologists—holds great promise for the field of planning. Indeed, the remarkable impact of transportation planners in planning and implementing the U.S. interstate highway network, as described in Chapter 2, undoubtedly is due to their development and use of systems analytical techniques.[15]

In conclusion, land use planning based on environmental landscape principles cannot reach its potential without utilizing the emerging technologies of data gathering, manipulation, analysis, and synthesis. The rest of the book presents various examples of these tools put specifically to work.

NOTES

1. M. Clawson and B. Held, *The Federal Lands: Their Use and Management* (Lincoln, Nebr.: University of Nebraska Press, 1957), p. 23.
2. U.S., Geological Survey, *U.S.G.S. History: Early History of the U.S.G.S.* (Washington, D.C.: U.S. Geological Survey Monographs of the United States Government, no. 1, Institute for Government Research, 1918), pp. 1-3.
3. Ibid., p. 6.
4. W. P. MacConnell, *Massachusetts Map Down,* Circular no. 169,

Massachusetts Agricultural Experimentation Station, Amherst, Massachusetts (1974).

5. D. C. Parker and M. F. Wolff, "Remote Sensing," in *The Surveillant Science: Remote Sensing of the Environment*,ed. R. K. Holz (Boston: Houghton Mifflin, 1973).

6. B. J. Niemann, Jr., M. M. McCarthy, S. A. Dunn, and F. Scharkne, "Satellite Sensing: Data from ERTS Will Revolutionize Decision around Us," *Landscape Architecture* 61, no 1, (October 1970):42-47.

7. Parker and Wolff, "Remote Sensing," p. 37.

8. D. Huff, *How to Lie with Statistics* (New York: W. W. Norton, 1954).

9. R. D. Remington and M. A. Schork, *Statistics with Application to Biological and Health Sciences* (Englewood, N.J.: Prentice-Hall, 1970), p. 2.

10. S. Siegel, *Nonparametric Statistics for the Behavioral Sciences* (New York: McGraw-Hill, 1956).

11. H. M. Proshansky, W. H. Ittelson, and L. G. Rivlin, *Environmental Psychology: Man and His Physical Setting* (New York: Holt, Rinehart and Winston, 1970).

12. E. H. Zube, R. Brush, and J. Gy. Fabos, *Landscape Assessment: Value Perceptions and Resources* (Stroudsburg, Pa.: Dowden, Hutchinson and Ross, 1975).

13. T. Murray, P. P. Sinton, and C. F. Steinitz, *Honey Hill: A System Analysis for Planning the Multiple Use of Controlled Water Area* (Springfield, Va.: National Technical Information Service, 1971).

14. K. H. Ferris and J. Gy. Fabos, *"Computechnics in the Landscape," Landscape Architecture* 65, no. 1 (January 1975):102-105.

15. D. E. Boyce, N. D. Day, and C. McDonald, *Metropolitan Plan Making*, (Philadelphia, Pa.: Regional Science Research Institute, 1970).

SUGGESTED READINGS

Books

Bross, I. D. *Design for Decision: An Introduction to Statistical Decision Making*. New York: Free Press, 1965.

Forrester, J. W., *Urban Dynamics*. Cambridge, Mass.: MIT Press, 1969.

Hillier, F. S., and Heberman, G. J. *Introduction to Operations Research*. San Francisco: Holden-Hay, 1967.

Holth, R. K., ed. *The Surveillant Science: Remote Sensing of the Environ-*

ment. Boston: Houghton-Mifflin, 1973.

Morse, P. M., ed. *Operations Research for Public Systems.* Cambridge, Mass.: MIT Press, 1967.

NASA, Scientific and Technical Information Facility, *Remote Sensing of Earth Resources: A Literature Survey with Indexes.* Washington, D.C., 1970.

Raser, J. F. *Simulation and Society: An Exploration of Scientific Gaming.* Boston: Allyn and Bacon, 1969.

Stoltenberg, C. H.; Ware, K. D.; Marty, R. J.; Wray, R. D.; and Wellons, J. D. *Planning Research for Resource Decisions.* Ames, Iowa: Iowa State University Press, 1970.

Westerlund, F. W. *Urban and Regional Planning Utilization of Remote Sensing Data: A Bibliography and Review of Pertinent Literature.* Springfield, Va.: National Technological Information Service, 1972.

Periodicals

The Annual of the Association of American Geographers. Association of American Geographers, Washington, D.C.

Computer and Information Systems. Cambridge Scientific Abstracts, Riverdale, Md.

Computer Graphics and Image Processing. Academic Press, New York.

Communications in Statistics. Marcel Decker, New York.

Data Management. Data Processing Management Assoc., Park Ridge, Ill.

Journal of the American Statistical Association. American Statistical Association, Washington, D.C.

Operational Research Quarterly. Pergamon Press, New York.

Photogrammetric Engineering. American Society of Photogrammetry, Falls Church, Va.

Remote Sensing of Environment. American Elsevier Publishing Co., New York.

PART 2

ENVIRONMENTAL ASSESSMENT PROCEDURES

INTRODUCTION

Three general types of environmental assessment techniques are discussed in the following chapters. These are resource, hazard, and development suitability assessments. The limitations of these techniques are discussed in a brief summary chapter together with some new developments in the area of environmental impact and ecological stability assessment. The focus here is on procedures that are useful for landscape planners in their efforts "to reconcile the needs of competing land uses and to incorporate them into a landscape in which man's civilization can prosper without destroying the natural and cultural resources on which societies are founded."[1] To achieve this aim, pertinent environmental data must be collected, analyzed, and assessed.

In the past, assessment techniques have often served as the basis for land use decisions. In many areas, for example, the real estate tax structure is based on the assessed value of a property or developed land use. In such instances, assessed value is influenced by factors such as size, location, or condition of the property as well as landscape and neighborhood quality. Some of these factors are easily quantifiable; others are highly qualitative. Both, however, provide useful information for planning and management considerations.

Unfortunately, until very recently, urbanization and metropolitanization have gone forward with little consideration for pertinent environmental values, thus causing valuable resources to be underutilized or destroyed and severe hazards to be suffered. The importance of a systematic assessment procedure of critical environmental factors has therefore become increasingly evident.

The general aim of the environmental assessment procedures that will be discussed here is to provide the following information: (1) an identification of significant environmental resources or land use constraints (e.g., water supply and floodplains); (2) an indication of the quality and quantity of each resource or constraint; (3) the location and distribution of each area of resource or constraint; and (4) an estimate of the potential impact of alternative uses on each resource or constraint area (e.g., suburban development over an aquifer area will probably significantly pollute existing groundwater unless precautions are taken). These types of assessments of environmental resource and hazard potential can provide decision makers with information useful in determining short-range and longer-range trade-offs to satisfy human objectives. An overall landscape planning process, which describes how these various environmental assessments can be used, is discussed in Part 3.

Each assessment chapter addresses a major environmental issue. The first deals with environmental resources, both with critical resources such as water and with less critical but important resources that enhance the quality of life, such as visual landscape quality. The second issue focuses on environmental constraints when neglected have a negative effect on public health, safety, or welfare. Both of these landscape parameters—resources and hazards—are assessed with a view toward preserving or protecting units of landscape from development. The third issue assesses those environmental attributes that can minimize the cost of developments while increasing human comfort and environmental amenities. This "developmental suitability" issue is concerned with recommending where development should occur. The fourth environmental issue deals with the concept of ecological stability and with the impairment of this stability due to development. A logical resolution of the first three issues may result in a land use configuration that could significantly impair the ecological balance or quality of a landscape. Impact and ecological assessments of proposed developments could help to estimate the potential impairment of proposed developments.

These chapters, therefore, briefly review the "state of the art" of assessment procedures in each of the four categories described. These procedures are treated in general terms. Although some of the assessment techniques are simple and may be adopted without much specialized training, many are complex and require significant training in disciplines such as geology or engineering. This great discrepancy of complexity among the various assessment techniques indeed suggests that some assessment techniques have been refined far more than others.

The following considerations have been used in organizing each of the chapters of Part 2. First, the reasons for the selection of each landscape attribute (e.g., water supply or visual quality) are presented. Then each attribute is briefly analyzed, and several relevant points are examined. These points are as follows: (1) the significance of each resource or hazard as seen by experts or other groups who have articulated its values; (2) a reference to the disciplines that deal with the assessment of each factor; (3) the data gathering, inventory, and classification procedures (if any) for each attribute; (4) the mapping scale or scales used for data gathering and inventory; (5) the estimated reliability of the data and inventory process; (6) the "state of the art" of the process of assessment of each attribute; (7) the estimated quality of each assessment process; (8) the time and money needed to assess each attribute; and (9) the acceptance and practical application of the assessment process by planners and decision makers.

Because the development of systematic landscape assessment is relatively new (especially with regard to several of the attributes), the answers to these questions sometimes represent only educated estimates. An attempt was made, however, to use the opinions of experts wherever possible.

NOTE

1. V. Vanicek, "Definition of Landscape Planning," *Landscape Planning* 1, no. 1 (June 1974).

5 ASSESSMENT OF LANDSCAPE RESOURCES

As noted in Chapter 2, the management of landscape resources is an important issue in metropolitan urban growth. The history of suburban expansion is replete with instances of unnecessary degradation and obliteration of valuable local resources. The effects of this shortsighted policy have been felt in both monetary and energy terms.

The first step in resolving these problems (or, rather, the second step—the first being the recognition of the problem) is clearly to identify the resources that have significance to contemporary metropolitan regions and to develop methods to assess their relative quantity, quality, and distribution in the regional landscape. This chapter outlines some of the techniques that have been designed for assessing metropolitan landscape resources. They include procedures for two renewable, or flow, resources (potable water and land productivity) and a depletable, or stock, resource (rock, sand, and gravel). There is also a description of methods for evaluating the so-called visual-cultural resources, such as visual quality.

ASSESSMENT OF POTABLE WATER RESOURCES

Water is essential to all forms of human activity. Nonetheless, the protection of local water supply sources has seldom been perceived as important by metropolitan planners, in large part because engineers have developed technically feasible means for transporting water over great distances at a reasonable cost. As this cost has risen significantly, however, many communities are again looking at various water supply alternatives.

Surface Water. It has been estimated that most of the water used by metropolitan populations is taken from surface water sources. Artificial impoundments, frequently located outside the boundaries of a metropolitan region, are the major source of water for most metropolises. The metropolitan region around Boston, for example, imports most of its drinking water from the Quabbin Reservoir, located some eighty miles away. There are several reasons why this type of importation is so common. Because the demand for metropolitan water is great, large land areas must be controlled. Impoundment sites and protected watersheds can be acquired far more easily outside of metropolitan growth areas where land values are lower. Water quality is also usually higher in these outlying areas, especially in hilly country that is relatively free of agricultural as well as urban uses.

The assessment of potential for surface water supply is a relatively complex procedure. It is most often undertaken collectively by geologists, engineers, soil scientists, resource economists, and landscape planners. Among the more significant physical variables in this assessment are the amount and quality of water available, topography, surficial and bedrock geology, erosion characteristics, evaporation rates, seismic hazards, and slope stability. In addition, several nonphysical factors such as projected need, costs, political acceptance, and environmental impact must be considered. A recent water resource assessment for the urbanized northeastern seaboard of the United States took six years to complete. It had a full-time staff of over thirty people, significant input from numerous federal and state agencies, and a budget of several million dollars.[1] In spite of this enormous effort, it provided only a "first-level" assessment within which more site-specific decisions could be made. Superregional water resources planning and implementation efforts such as this will undoubtedly continue. Nevertheless, the potential of local potable groundwater supplies within metropolitan regions is being increasingly considered as a viable alternative to regional solutions.

Groundwater Supply (Quantity). Recent studies suggest that in many regions, the supply of water from local underground sources is significantly less expensive than imported surface water. Sommers estimates that groundwater, where available, can be developed for one-tenth the cost of surface water.[2] A 1972 economic study concluded that local groundwater in the northeastern United States could be utilized at one-third to one-fifth of the cost of imported water.[3] At the same time, interest in groundwater has expanded as increasing numbers of large-yield wells have been successfully brought into operation.

The related disciplines of geology and hydrology have significantly expanded our ability to search out large quantities of groundwater. Surficial geologic mapping and classification schemes have aided the development of a more specialized groundwater classification and evaluation system. These schemes are based on an understanding of the geologic formations that permit the infiltration of water through the upper layers of the ground and those that retain the water that filters down.

Significant water-retaining aquifers have three attributes. The porous material should be extensive, both in thickness and in area; the water table should be high; and the amount of natural recharge should be extensive. In simplified terms, the quantitative assessment of groundwater potential is based on an analysis of these three attributes.

Although many techniques are used in assessing groundwater, they may be grouped into four basic types: remote sensing techniques, surficial geologic techniques, on-site geophysical interpretive techniques, and on-site subsurface techniques. Remote sensing can give a general idea about groundwater through specialized thermal or infrared reconnaissance.[4] These techniques are especially useful for inaccessible areas where the surficial geology has not yet been mapped. They provide an initial estimate of groundwater potential, which must be followed up by more accurate on-site assessment.

Surficial geologic techniques are most frequently used in metropolitan regions where geological maps are often available. One typical accepted technique for groundwater resources is the "Connecticut Method" used in southeastern New England. This approach correlates groundwater yield with the percentage of stratified drift within a basin.[5] Using simple correlation techniques, higher water supply probabilities are attached to porous surface materials such as sand and gravel. In addition, a value is given to the potential storage capacity or volume of these aquifers. From rainfall records and land use or vegetation cover, scientists estimate the recharge potential of the watershed area. This technique yields satisfactory results in areas that are mapped with surficial geologic information. In areas where only soil data are available, detailed soil maps may be used—if it is realized that the result will be less accurate.

The "Connecticut Method" and similar surficial assessments can be followed up by more accurate on-site geophysical investigation. Several methods, which were originally developed for the exploration of petroleum and other minerals, are available, including gravitational, seismic, and electrical techniques. In the most accurate (and costly) technique, a subsurface method, i.e., the drilling of test wells, is used. A pump test is run for each well which provides precise data in determining safe yield transmissibility and other properties.

Recently, local town planners have begun to consider groundwater potential in their municipal areas. This trend can be traced in some measure to the failure of large regional systems to provide adequate water for the increasing metropolitan population. Indeed, much of the growth in metropolitan areas has occurred outside of the older, established metropolitan water districts. Some of these newer, decentralized settlements are less amenable to the regional systems approach. Many communities are finding that there is an added benefit from exploiting local groundwater sources: protected aquifers and aquifer recharge areas may also be used for recreation.

Groundwater Supply (Quality). The quality of drinking water has a direct impact on health, and much of the research on water quality standards has been conducted by the public health–related disciplines: environmental science (microbiology), environmental engineering, and general public health planning. The research has developed ten critical parameters for water quality assessment: pathogens, phosphates, nitrates, pesticides, petroleum, lead, miscellaneous industrial wastes, sediments, radioactivity, and heat. In many localities, public water supplies are now being developed that are free from these pollutants, or else they are being treated to mitigate these pollution problems.

The technology has been available for many years to convert even sewage to drinkable water. Yet this type of recycling has not received wide public acceptance. An alternative approach to extensive treatment (especially because some pollutants are not easily treated) is being investigated by several planners, namely, the regulation of the use of land in aquifer recharge areas to exclude polluting uses.

The effect of land use on groundwater quality can also be used in the assessment of potential water sources. The Careaga technique, for instance, analyzes land use type, intensity of development, and soil type to estimate the probable quality of any water that may be found underground.[6] Analyses of this kind provide generally accurate assessments, which are useful in establishing relatively prudent planning guidelines.

As indicated in the introduction to Part 2, each assessment technique will be illustrated with an example. Since new large surface water supply sources are usually located outside of the metropolitan region, only the groundwater quantity and quality assessment are shown below. The following example is reproduced from the METLAND landscape research study at the

University of Massachusetts. The town of Burlington, Masssachusetts, was selected to illustrate the assessment of groundwater quantity and quality. Figure 19 shows the location and size of Burlington in relation to the large Boston metropolitan region. Figure 20 illustrates the results of the application of the groundwater assessment technique to the town. (Most of the following assessment procedures use Burlington or its neighbor, Wilmington, Massachusetts, as examples.)

ASSESSMENT OF LAND PRODUCTIVITY

Two aspects of land productivity have been selected for this review. The first of these is agricultural productivity. The preservation of prime soils for farming has traditionally received little attention, especially in the United States, where agricultural output has occasionally been so plentiful that the federal government has paid money to farmers not to plant. However, inherently productive land is becoming increasingly more important, especially when it is found within expanding metropolitan regions.[7] Agricultural land is ordinarily easy to develop, and in this country over a million acres per year are converted to nonfarm uses. The trend is changing, however, as worldwide food shortages and food price increases have given rise to a new concern for preserving agricultural land within metropolitan regions.

The second aspect of land productivity considers the land's potential to support wildlife. For several years, governmental efforts to control hunting activities have led to the protection and management of some wildlife species. During the past twenty years, however, various environmental organizations have helped to increase the general public interest in the protection of wildlife for recreation such as birdwatching or, indeed, merely for its own sake. The interest in wildlife has also increased as a result of the recent ecology movement.[8]

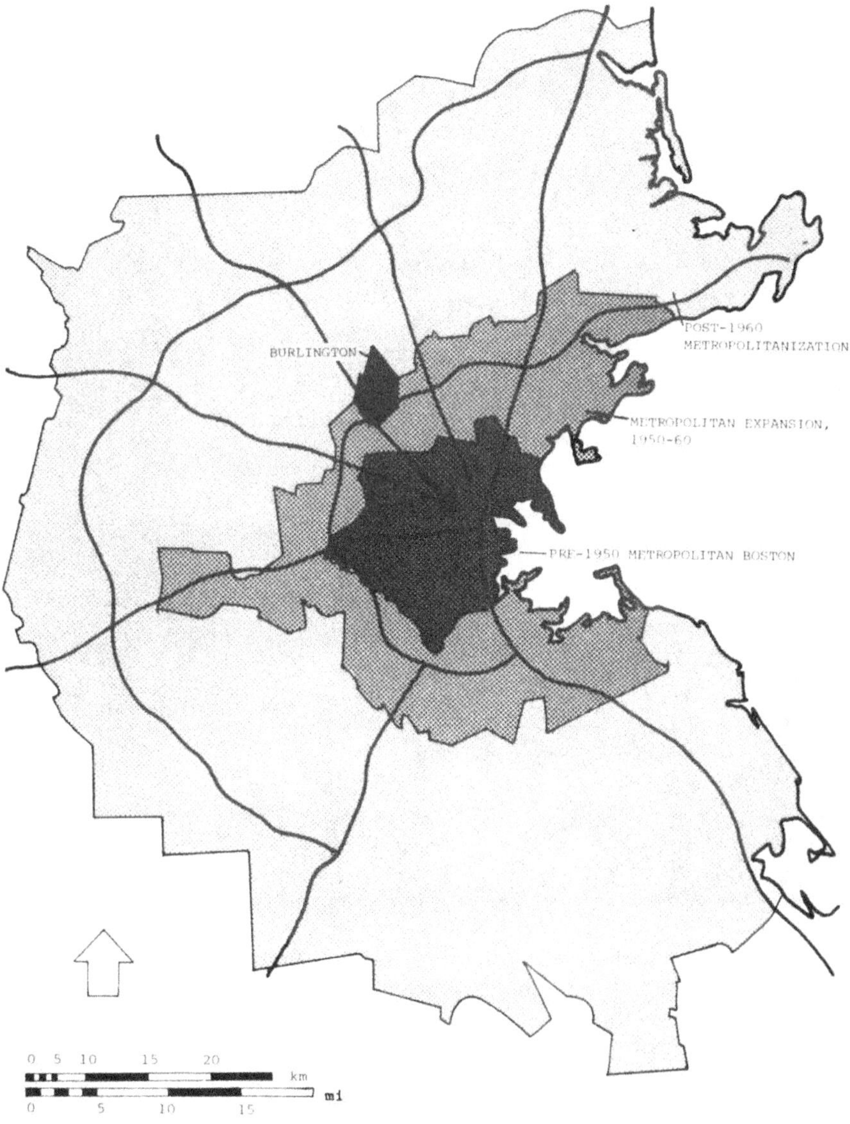

FIGURE 19. The location of the town of Burlington is shown in relation to the larger Boston metropolitan region. This town site is used to illustrate the special resource value, hazard, and development suitability assessment procedures. Notice that the town of Burlington has been subjected to pressures of metropolitanization since the 1950s.

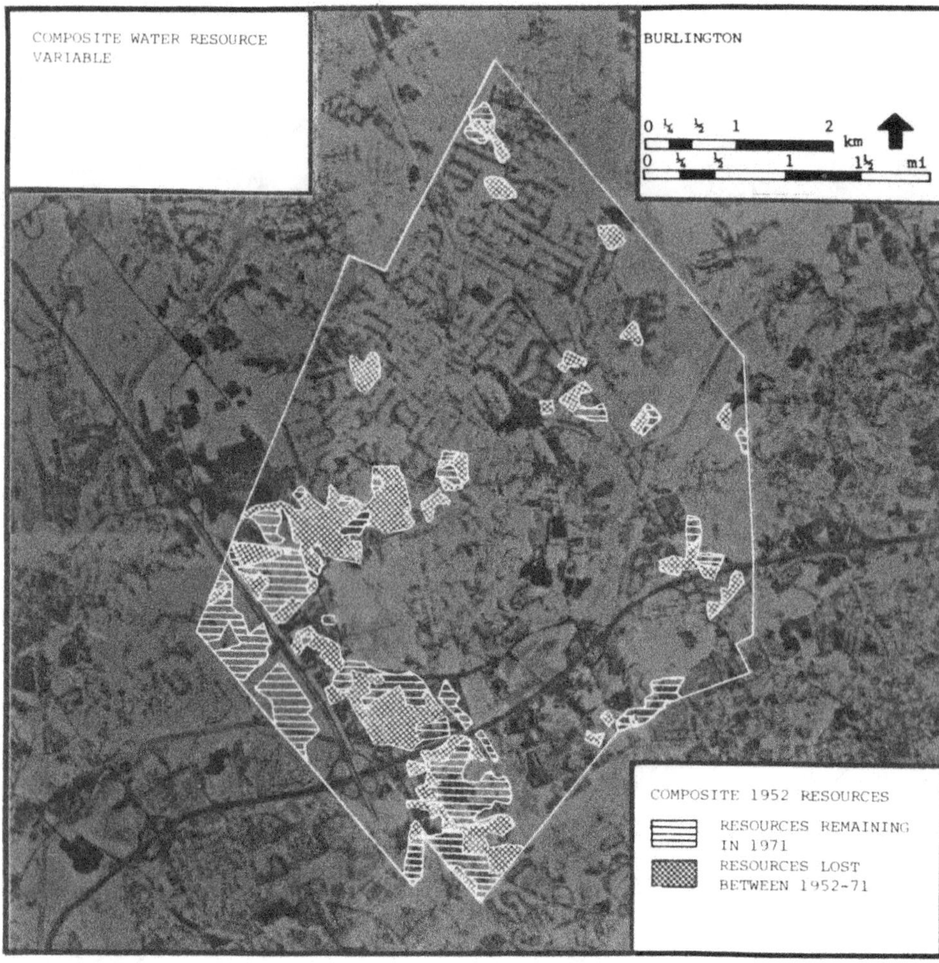

FIGURE 20. A comparison of the water resource assessment results when applied to a community subject to heavy metropolitan growth pressures from 1952 to 1971. Note the value change that occurred (see legend). In the southwest portion of the town, the area of highest water resource quality and supply in 1952, significant resource value loss occurred. The location of a large highway generated shopping center and industrial and residential developments in this high-value area, thereby eliminating a significant percentage of the approximately two square miles of high-value water resources potential. Instances of this type frequently force these developing communities to import water in the future at a higher cost.

The assessment process was developed by Richard Careaga and Susan Cole, environmental geologists at the University of Massachusetts landscape research group. The process evaluates the pollution effects of various land use types and the relative impermeability of soil and land use types as well as the effects of evapotranspiration on water resource quality and supply.

Agricultural Productivity Assessment. Over the past seventy to eighty years, soil scientists have developed and refined a body of accurate techniques for the classification and assessment of soils. General assessment techniques, based primarily on remote sensing data, are now used in many developed countries. By corroborating remote sensing data with rigorous field investigation, a more detailed soil survey can also be produced, one that is accurate to a scale of one hectare (2.4 acres). In this country, the tasks of both detailed and general soil assessment are carried out by the Soil Conservation Service (SCS), an agency of the U.S. Department of Agriculture.

The SCS evaluates a variety of soil characteristics. Among the ratings it regularly assigns is an estimate of the "capability" of the soil to support agricultural production. Eight capability classes are used, ranging from most productive to least productive. These classes are based on such parameters as slope, moisture holding capability, erosion characteristics, texture, structure, and drainage characteristics.

The SCS agricultural capability assessment is based solely on soil characteristics. Several landscape planners have expanded this procedure to include a consideration of present land use. The reason for this is simple. Although soil studies may suggest that an area's soil can sustain high agricultural productivity, if the land is developed for a nonagricultural use, such as housing, it will probably never be used for agriculture.

Detailed soil studies are available for most of the metropolitan regions of the United States. In Massachusetts, for instance, the majority of planning consultants preparing a community master plan have access to detailed soil data. The way these data are used, however, often varies considerably. For example, the most productive soils are also excellent leaching fields for on-site sewage disposal. Many planners therefore recommend such areas for higher-density residential use. The result is a further loss of highly productive agricultural lands. Nevertheless, because of the increased attention to agricultural productivity in metropolitan landscapes, assessment techniques that evaluate metropolitan landscapes in terms of inherent soil productivity and in terms of how existing land uses detract from that productive potential are becoming more important. Figure 21 shows how such a technique has been applied to Burlington, Massachusetts.

Wildlife Productivity Assessment. The science of wildlife biology provides detailed information on most wildlife species. Wildlife biologists have ascertained, for example, that the most pertinent characteristics of good wildlife habitat are climate, soil productivity, and vegetative conditions. When considering a given metropolitan region, climate may be considered constant. Vegetation conditions, however, usually depend on land use and management practices. It is therefore likely that soil productivity and existing land use will be the crucial parameters that determine the potential quantity and quality of wildlife in a metropolitan area.

If these are indeed the crucial parameters, assessment techniques can help identify landscape areas that should be protected because of their high wildlife productivity. This approach, which protects existing resources, is significantly different from the nineteenth-century concept of park planning, in which a bit of nature was re-created within urban areas in the form of a park.

Figure 22 shows the results of the application of a wildlife assessment technique. If detailed soil data are available, this technique will provide pertinent wildlife information inexpensively. Obviously, it should be followed up by more detailed studies to determine the precise wildlife values of specific areas with a high potential for wildlife productivity.

ASSESSMENT OF EARTH RESOURCES (ROCK, SAND, AND GRAVEL)

The scarcity of earth resources required for urban construction activities was not a problem until the late 1940s. Before that period, most cities and metropolises grew in smaller, more concentrated

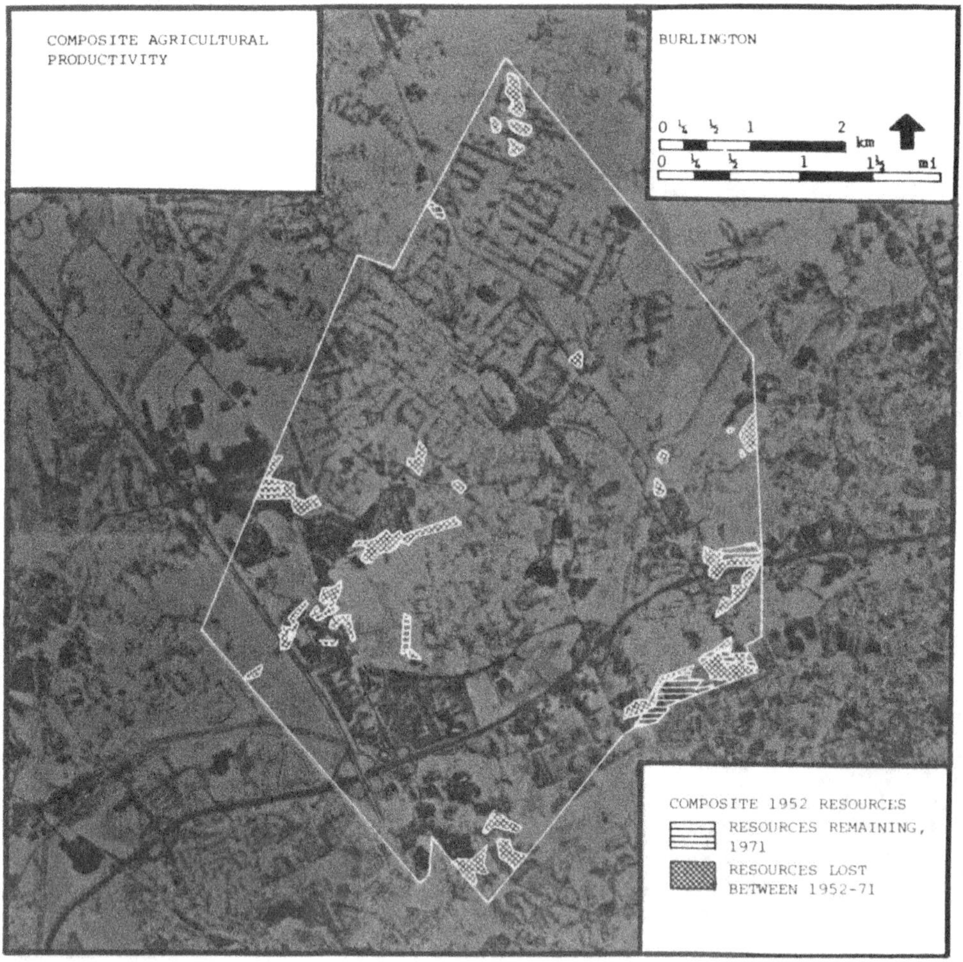

FIGURE 21. A comparison of the agricultural productivity assessment results when applied to a community subject to heavy metropolitan growth pressures from 1952 to 1971. Because of the extreme scarcity of prime agricultural soils in this community, few prime agricultural areas existed even in 1952. The process of urbanization, however, all but eliminated agriculture from this community by 1971, as the figure shows. The elimination of prime agricultural soils from the metropolitan region is a critical problem in terms of the region's relative agricultural self-sufficiency, in terms of the quantity of prime soils nationwide, and in terms of increasing transportation costs to truck in agricultural produce.

The assessment process was developed by Stephanie Williston and later revised by Stephanie Caswell, resource specialists and planners of the University of Massachusetts landscape research group. The process uses the USDA Soil Conservation Service's soil survey, which ranks the relative productivity of different soil types; it also includes an analysis of the detractor effects of varying land use types on potential agricultural productivity.

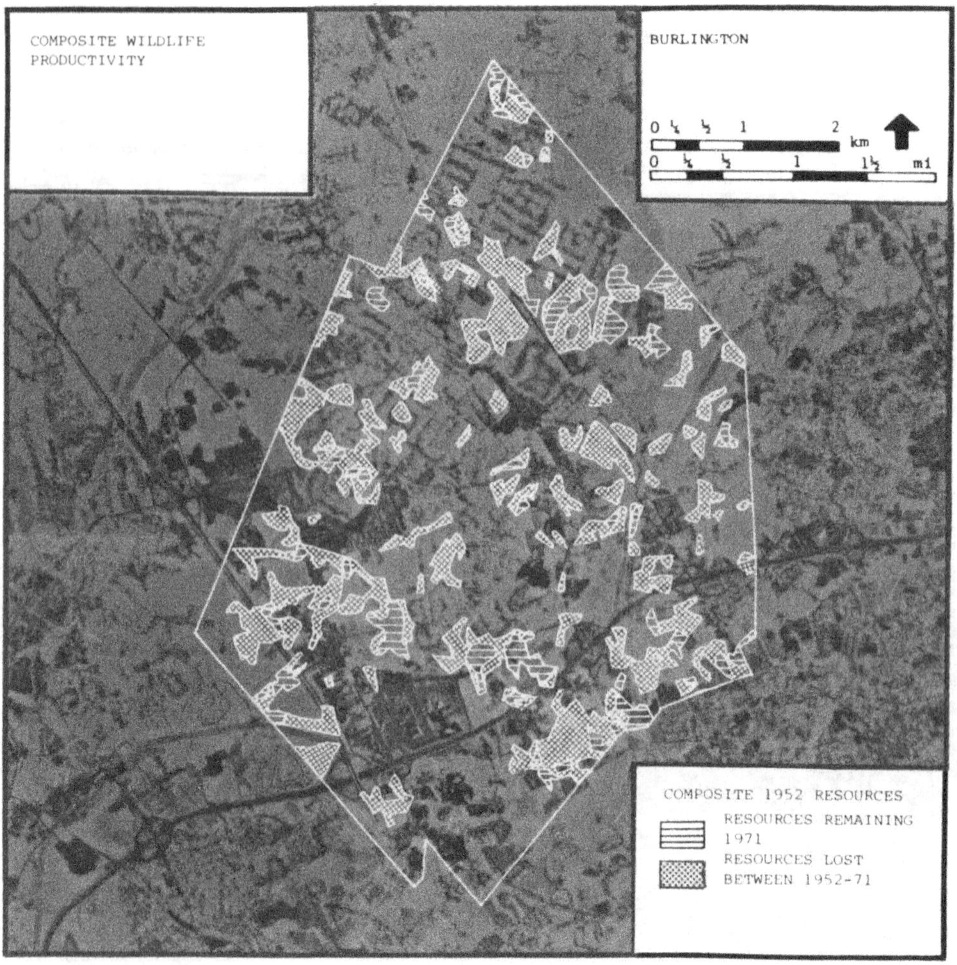

FIGURE 22. A comparison of the wildlife productivity assessment results when applied to a community subject to heavy metropolitan growth pressures from 1952 to 1971. It is readily apparent that more areas have potential wildlife suitability than had agricultural suitability, as may be seen by comparing this figure with Figure 21. The differences stem from farming's need for prime soils on level land; wildlife needs are far less stringent. In addition, wetland areas, generally not suitable for agriculture, are highly productive in terms of wildlife. Another reason that more wildlife areas appear is the adaptability of several wildlife species to the urbanizing environment.

The assessment process was developed by Stephanie Williston and later revised by Stephanie Caswell, resource specialists and planners of the University of Massachusetts landscape research group. This process uses the USDA Soil Conservation Service's soil survey, which ranks the potential wildlife habitat of different soil types; it also includes an analysis of the detractor effects of varying land use types on potential combined wetland, woodland, and openland wildlife productivity.

areas. Immediately adjacent to these areas, sand, gravel, and other aggregate material could often be found in abundance. But most contemporary metropolitan regions have increased in area from ten to fifteen times over, and many of these sources have been eliminated. The construction of housing, schools, industries, or shopping centers on the land that overlay these deposits made many of them absolutely inaccessible. But even building close to them indirectly eliminated potential quarry sites, because the localized noise and dust associated with mining activities would be unacceptable to the new nearby residents.

Two factors exacerbate the problem of earth resource supply. First, metropolitan areas need enormous quantities of these materials for the construction and maintenance of roads, buildings, and airports. Second, because of the great bulk of earth resources, transportation costs rapidly increase with distance hauled. It is estimated that after twenty-five miles, transportation costs equal or exceed the cost of extracting the rock at the quarry.[9] Increased transportation also adds to other environmental problems such as noise and air pollution.

The assessment techniques for the various types of earth resources are similar. They are therefore discussed here as one type of assessment, with a note to identify the differences among them. Geology is the principle discipline with expertise in assessing earth resources, although some soil scientists estimate sand and gravel potential based on soil surveys. Only the geologist's approach is discussed here. Geologists have developed a three-level assessment technique that is analogous to the assessment technique used for groundwater supply. The three-level technique includes a general survey, followed by site-specific seismic tests, and finally, a site-specific sampling of core borings to verify quantity, distribution, and quality.

The general survey is the most useful for planning in metropolitan areas. Because only about 20 percent of metropolitan regions are actually developed with housing, industry, and commercial uses, the protection of all potential earth resource sites is often appropriate, at least until further detailed studies determine their precise quality. This general assessment is a simple process and can be accomplished inexpensively. The location of various earth resources such as granite, basalt, sand, and gravel is determined by analyzing two pieces of generally available information: surficial geologic maps and local geologic history. If this information is not available, the various remote sensing devices on field surveys (Chapter 4) can often provide much of the basic information needed for this general level of assessment.

In either case, geologists can use these data to estimate the location and the probable quantity of earth resources. Furthermore, they can usually make inferences about the quality of deposits as well. The existing land use of the site and its surrounding area can then be analyzed to get an indication of the practical feasibility of quarrying. Finally, existing and proposed highways and roads are analyzed to determine the feasibility of access to the site. The application of a sand and gravel assessment technique to the town of Burlington, Massachusetts, is shown in Figure 23.

It should be noted that sand and gravel deposits are often high-quality aquifers and aquifer recharge areas as well. The excavation of these resources, therefore, may decrease both the quality and quantity of the local groundwater supply. Earth resource assessment is only one consideration that must be used in conjunction with several others to determine optional land use and management practices. The most immediate problem in many metropolitan regions, however, is a lack of sufficient information on where their earth resources are located. Planners often assume that workable earth resource deposits are plentiful, which, as we have seen, is not necessarily so. To minimize future increases in cost, energy consumption, and environmental pollution, it is important that each landscape pressured by metropolitanization be assessed at least to this first level, so that potential rock, sand, and gravel areas can be protected. The assessment techniques of earth resource scientists are well developed, but planners have made limited use of them. This should be rectified without delay.

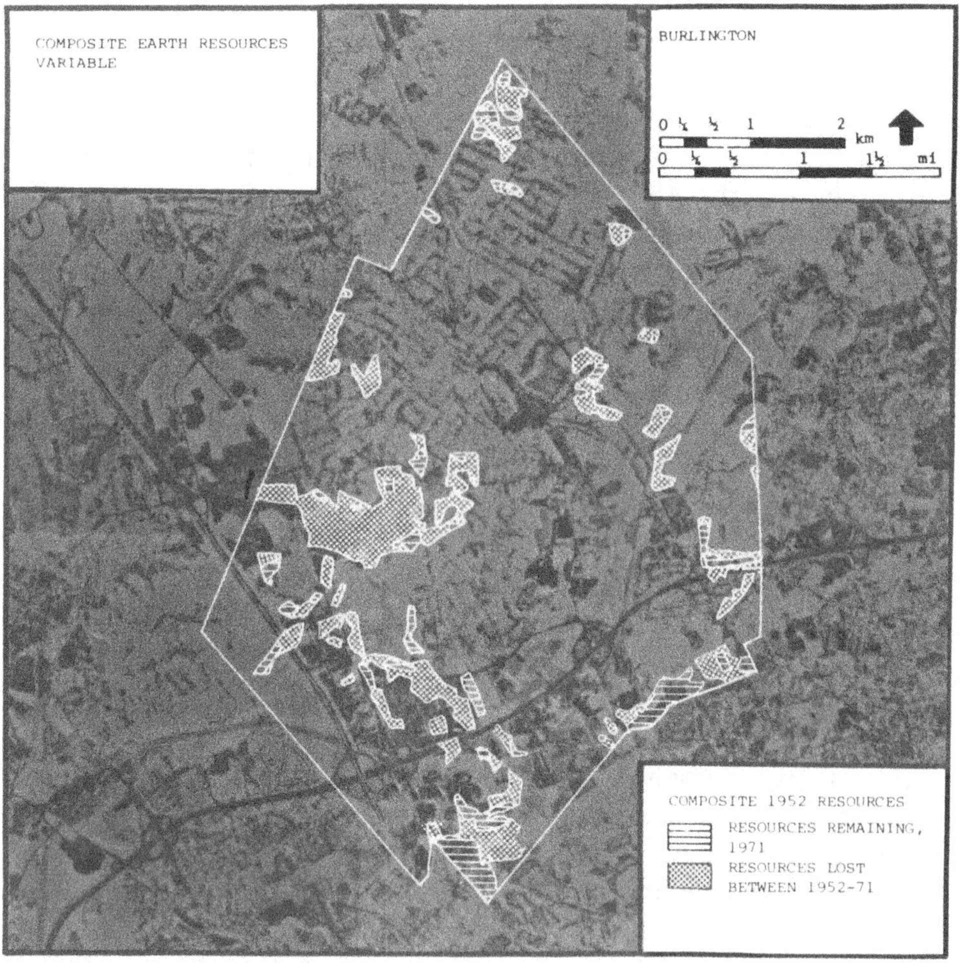

FIGURE 23. A comparison of the earth resource assessment results when applied to a comunity subject to heavy metropolitan growth pressures from 1952 to 1971. Sand and gravel resources are an essential element of the urbanization process. Significant sand and gravel resource areas of 1952, in the western part of the community, were effectively eliminated by 1971 by the location of industrial and residential development generated by the intersection of two superhighways in these prime resource areas. The elimination of this resource, which is as necessary for maintenance as for initial construction, will force the community to import this resource at a substantial transportation cost.

The assessment process was developed by Susan Cole, environmental geologist of the University of Massachusetts landscape research group. The process uses the USDA Soil Conservation Service's soil survey, which (or surficial geology maps) details sand and gravel resource potential. In addition, land use detractor ratings are used to determine the feasibility of resource extraction.

ASSESSMENT OF VISUAL-CULTURAL VALUES

Human society has long valued the aesthetic aspects of the environment. We admire the elegance of cathedrals, the awesome grandeur of the Alps, and the exalting stature of the California redwoods. As a result, we have often taken measures to protect these outstanding landscape features for all to appreciate.

The sprawling metropolitan areas of today may not have many of these spectacular features; nonetheless, they undoubtedly have many beautiful areas, such as riverfronts, lakes, diversely patterned wetlands, and romantic town commons, which are valued highly by residents throughout the region and whose preservation would be widely endorsed. The question for land use planners becomes: if these aesthetic and cultural resources are valued, how can they be identified and protected?

The discipline that has focused on these issues for many years and that has developed techniques for assessing aesthetic values in the environment is landscape architecture. This profession has been aided by various historians, philosophers, and environmental psychologists. Most of the behavioral studies and assessment techniques developed by these researchers focus on two significant variables: landscape complexity and visual-cultural compatibility.[10]

The value of landscape complexity has been supported by numerous researchers,[11] who have found that more complex landscapes are both more pleasing and more interesting to people. There are several ways of evaluating environmental complexity from a visual perspective. Many assessment techniques attempt to measure the *contrast* between landscape elements. Contrast is one of the main distinguishing features in any visual stimulus. In the landscape, it is usually provided by topography, water, vegetation, and the pattern of land use. *Diversity* is also an important component of complexity and is often measured in terms of the number of different land uses in a given area.[12] Using these perceived values, landscape architects can identify metropolitan areas that possess high visual contrast and diversity or that have unique cultural values. These are termed high-quality visual areas.[13]

Visual compatibility is probably less widely measured than landscape complexity. Only recently have studies undertaken to discover to what degree a neighboring land use or activity may enhance or detract from the perceived quality of a given area.[14] According to one study, visual land use compatibility explains one's perception of visual quality more than any other visual variable does.[15]

Although supporting evidence from the behavioral sciences has improved visual-cultural assessment techniques, they are still significantly less dependable than the other assessment techniques reviewed in this chapter. Nonetheless, landscape architects have developed several normative assessment techniques that seem to provide acceptable estimates of the relative values of visual and cultural qualities.[16] For generalized assessments, they often use topographic maps, land use maps, and air photos. Site inspections to verify the mapped information are also common. Occasionally, a representative cross section of the resident population of the assessed areas will be tested through photographs to corroborate the values of the professional assessors.

Figure 24 shows the application of a visual resource value assessment technique. Because there are no significant visual resource areas within Burlington (the town used in previous examples), the island of Nantucket was selected to illustrate a visual assessment technique.

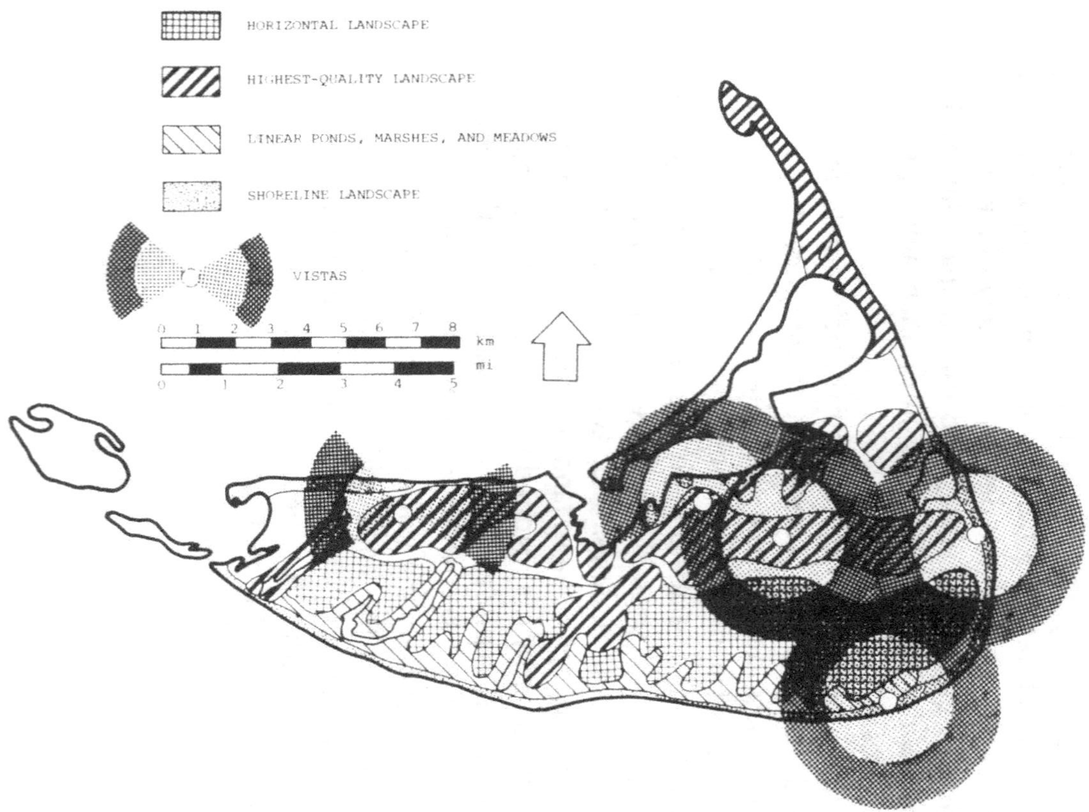

FIGURE 24. This figure illustrates the significant visual quality and scenic view areas of the island of Nantucket. This visual assessment was prepared in 1966 by the author in collaboration with Dr. Ervin Zube, study coordinator. The process identified significant island landscape types of high scenic quality. These landscapes were ranked according to their perceived value for public use and to insure their preservation and protection for future use.

NOTES

1. North Atlantic Regional Water Resources Study Coordinating Committee, *North Atlantic Regional Water Resources Study* (Washington, D.C.: U.S. Government Printing Office, 1971).

2. D. Sommers, "Put Hydrology into Planning," *Ground Water* 8, no. 6 (1970):4.

3. T. Gupta, "A Multivariate Model for Public Management of Freshwater Wetlands" (Ph.D. Diss., University of Massachusetts, Amherst, 1972.

4. W. M. Adams et al., "A Hydrogeophysical Survey Using Remote-Sensing Methods from Kawaihea to Kailua-Kona, Hawaii," *Ground Water* 9 (January-February 1971):42-50.

5. M. A. Cervione, *Water Resources of Connecticut, Part 6 Upper Housatonic River Basin,* State of Connecticut, Connecticut Water Resource Bulletin no 21., 1972.

6. J. Gy. Fabos, *Model for Landscape Assessment: Part I of the "Metropolitan Landscape Planning Model" (METLAND),* Research Bulletin no. 602, University of Massachusetts, Agricultural Experiment Station, Amherst, Massachusetts, 1973, pp. 53-55.

7. J. Gottman, *Megalopolis: The Urbanized Northeastern Seaboard of the United States* (Cambridge, Mass.: MIT Press, 1961), p. 261.

8. E. P. Odum, *Ecology* (New York: Holt, Rinehart and Winston, 1963).

9. W. J. Keating, "Symposium on Quarrying in Massachusetts," in *Economic Geology in Massachusetts,* ed. O. C. Farguhar (Amherst, Mass.: University of Massachusetts Press, 1967).

10. E. H. Zube, R. O. Brush, and J. Gy. Fabos, *Landscape Assessment: Values, Perceptions and Resources* (Stroudsburg, Pa.: Dowden, Hutchinson and Ross, 1975).

11. D. F. Berlyne, "Complexity and Incongruity Variables as Determinants of Exploratory Choice and Evaluating Ratings," *Canadian Journal of Psychology* 22, no. 3 (1963):274-289; P. C. Vitz, "Preference for Different Amount of Visual Complexity," *Behavioral Science* 11 (1966):105-114; H. Day, "Evaluations of Subjective Complexity, Pleasingness and Interestingness for a Series of Random Polygons Varying in Complexity," *Perception and Psychophysics* 2 (1967):281-286; R. R. Terwillinger, "Pattern of Complexity and Affective Arousal," *Perceptual and Motor Skills* 17 (1963):387-395; D. deJonge, "Applied Hodology," *Landscape* 17, no. 2 (1967-1968):10-11.

12. B. Pyron, "Form and Diversity in Human Habits: Judgemental and Attitude Responses," *Environment and Behavior* 4, no. 1 (1972):87-120.

13. R. J. Riotte, J. Gy. Fabos, and E. H. Zube, "Model for Evaluation of

the Visual-Cultural Resources of the Southeastern New England Region," in Zube, Brush, and Fabos, *Landscape Assessment.*

14. W. G. Hendrix and J. Gy. Fabos, "Visual Land Use Compatibility as a Significant Contributor to Visual Resource Quality," *International Journal of Environment Studies* 1, (1975):1-8.

15. E. H. Zube, D. G. Pitt, and T. W. Anderson, *Perception and Measurement of Scenic Resources in the Southern Connecticut River Valley,* Publication no. R-74-1, Institute for Man and His Environment, University of Massachusetts, Amherst, 1974, pp. 112-113.

16. Riotte, Fabos, and Zube, "Model for Evaluation"; R. C. Smardon, "Assessing Visual-Cultural Values of Inland Wetlands in Massachusetts," in Zube, Brush, and Fabos, *Landscape Assessment.*

SUGGESTED READINGS

Bartelli, L. J., et al., eds. *Soil Surveys and Land Use Planning.* Madison, Wis.: Soil Science Society of America and American Society of Agronomy, 1966.

Bates, R. L. *Geology of the Industrial Rocks and Minerals.* New York: Dover Publications, 1969.

Bireland, P. W. *Pedology Weathering and Geomorphological Research.* New York: Oxford University Press, 1974.

Brady, N. C. *The Nature and Properties of Soils.* 8th ed. New York: Macmillan, 1974.

Buckman, H. O., and Brady, N. C. *The Nature and Properties of Soils.* New York: Macmillan, 1969.

Coates, D. R. *Environmental Geomorphology and Landscape Evaluation.* Stroudsburg, Pa.: Dowden, Hutchinson and Ross, 1972.

Davis, S. M., and DeWeist, R. J. *Hydrology.* New York: Harper and Row, 1970.

Donahue, R. L. *Our Soils and Their Management: Increasing Production through Soil and Water Conservation.* 3rd ed. Danville, Ill.: Interstate, 1970.

Fitzpatrick, E. A. *Pedology: A Systematic Approach to Soil Science.* Edinburgh: Oliver and Boyd, 1971.

Flawn, P. T. *Environmental Geology.* New York: Harper and Row, 1970.

Foth, H. D., and Turk, L. M. *Fundamentals of Soil Science.* 5th ed. New York: John Wiley and Sons, 1972.

Krutilla, J., ed. *Natural Environments: Studies in Theoretical and Applied Analysis.* Baltimore: Johns Hopkins University Press, 1972.

Leopold, L. *Water, A Primer.* New York: D. H. Freeman, 1974.

Stewart, G. A., ed. *Land Evaluation.* South Melbourne: The MacMillan Company of Australia, 1968.

Tobb, D. D. *Ground Water Hydrology.* New York: John Wiley and Sons, 1959.

Walton, W. C. *Ground Water Resource Evaluation.* New York: McGraw-Hill, 1970.

Zube, E. H.; Brush, R. O.; and Fabos, J. Gy. *Landscape Assessment: Values, Perceptions and Resources.* Stroudsburg, Pa.: Dowden, Hutchinson and Ross, 1975.

Periodicals

General:

Landscape Architecture Quarterly. American Society of Landscape Architects, McLean, Va.

Soils:

Agriculture. Corporation des Agronomes de la Province de Quebec, Montreal, Quebec, Canada

Agricultural Engineering. American Society of Agricultural Engineers, Joseph, Mich.

Agricultural Science. Academy of Agricultural Science, Sofia, Bulgaria.

Agronomy News. American Society of Agronomy, Madison, Wis.

Agronomy Journal. American Society of Agronomy, Madison, Wis.

Congresses of the International Society of Soil Scientists. International Society of Soil Science, Amsterdam, Netherlands.

Environmental Science and Technology. American Chemical Society, Washington, D.C.

Proceedings of the Soil Science Society of America. Soil Science Society of America, Madison, Wis.

Soil Science. Williams and Wilkins Co., Baltimore, Md.

Visual:

Behavioral Science. Health Science Center Library, University of Louisville, Louisville, Ky.

Environment and Behavior. Sage Publications, Beverly Hills, Calif.

Journal of Forestry. Society of American Foresters, Washington, D.C.

Water:

Ground Water. Water Well Journal Publishing Co., Columbus, Ohio.

Ground Water Age. Elmhurst, Ill.
Journal of Soil and Water Conservation. Soil Conservation Society of America, Ankey, Iowa.
Water Resources Research. American Water Resources Assoc., Washington, D.C.

6 ASSESSMENT OF LANDSCAPE HAZARDS

This chapter is concerned with environmental circumstances that cause significant harm to people and property. As noted in Chapter 2, these "landscape hazards" can be grouped into two categories. In the first category are the hazards caused by natural phenomena that are harmful only when human activity gets in their way. The most important hazards in this category are flooding, landslides, and earthquakes. The second category includes hazards generated by human action, such as air pollution and noise pollution. Although there is considerable knowledge about each of these hazards, the damage resulting from them has increased significantly during the nineteenth and twentieth centuries.[1]

In the case of natural hazards, two reasons for this increase can be discerned. First, people tend to "get into nature's way" in the pursuit of various essential human objectives. For example, human society has traditionally depended on rivers and streams as sources of transportation and power. As a result, development often occurs in the areas adjacent to rivers, even though periodically severe flooding is inevitable.

Second, potential natural hazards tend to be ignored because they occur infrequently. Most major floods occur at intervals of twenty to fifty years. Although concern is usually intense immediately after a disastrous flood, a short time later it is all but forgotten.[2]

Our perception of hazards generated directly by human action is just as inadequate. Many of these hazards increase incrementally, and we tend not to notice them. The widening of a highway, for example, or the lengthening of an airport runway is usually thought of as an improvement in the transportation infrastructure. The urban development that takes place around highways and airports, however, is also the result of similar incremental decisions. When viewed comprehensively, the growth of a town from six thousand people to twenty thousand in fifteen years can easily be credited with causing a major increase in air or noise pollution. But public concern about the prospect of increased pollution is usually expressed only when one particularly noticeable project is proposed. The smaller incremental changes are missed.

Measurement, evaluation, and assessment techniques for flooding and air and noise pollution are well developed, but many of them are used to determine "corrective" actions aimed at ameliorating existing hazards. The primary focus here will be on those assessment techniques developed to *prevent* potential hazards from affecting people or property by using landscape and land use planning techniques.

NATURAL HAZARDS

Flooding, landslides, and earthquakes are among the most damaging hazards that affect urbanized regions. They often occur in combination. In drier climatic regions, for example, when heavy rains hit unstable soils, flooding will be accompanied by landslides. This is particularly true when the natural surface of the ground has been disturbed by human activity, such as overgrazing or development. Similarly, earthquakes often generate severe landslides and may be combined with flooding due to dam failure. Although these events often occur simultaneously, a separate discussion on each is useful to identify the areas that are particularly subject to the individual hazards.

Flooding. Of the three natural hazards discussed here, flooding is the most ubiquitous and damaging in a metropolitan region. Until recently, the most common flood-control measures have been dikes and levees or the straightening and "channelizing" of meandering watercourses in the lower reaches of a stream. Dams have been built in upstream areas to create artificial lakes, which are intended to retain large amounts of water generated suddenly by melting snow or heavy rain. Other engineering solutions include the waterproofing of buildings or the construction of only those types of structures (such as concrete garages) that are not damaged by flooding and over which apartment buildings or offices may be built without being exposed to a flood hazard.

Recently, however, several nonphysical flood prevention devices have been increasingly used. Geologists and hydrologists have greatly improved the accuracy of mapping floodplain boundaries. In response, many communities and states, aware of the probability and consequences of flooding, are now protecting floodplains from development by housing, industrial, or commercial uses. Many planners have adopted the one-hundred-year floodplain as a standard for protection and recommend that development be permitted only outside these floodplain boundaries.

There are two basic problems, however, with this new planning norm. The first problem stems from the misleading nature of the term *hundred-year floodplain.* A hundred-year flood does not necessarily occur every one hundred years. Rather, it is a flood of a magnitude whose *probability* of occurring *in any one year* is a hundred to one. There is no reason why a hundred-year (or 1 percent probability) flood cannot occur in consecutive years. It is unlikely, but it can happen—and has happened.

The second problem with flood probability assessment is that floodplains increase in size as urbanization increases. This is due to several factors. Many physical flood-control devices, for instance, transfer the problem of flooding to other portions of a river basin. The utilization of dikes, levees, and floodwalls decreases the floodplain's capacity for holding floodwater. Consequently, in areas located upstream from these physical structures, the flood level will rise even higher, thus extending the area subject to flood. Second, buildings and roads situated on a floodplain decrease the amount of floodwater that can soak into the ground. This raises the level of the flood and therefore the area that is flooded.[3] Recent studies have shown that even lower-density suburban development significantly increases the impermeability of a floodplain. Development at a density of five dwelling units per acre (about twelve dwelling units per hectare) covers an estimated 32 percent of the surface with roofs and pavement.[4]

The data-gathering techniques used by hydrologists to determine flood hazard potential are simple. Climatic data on the distribution, intensity, and other pertinent aspects of rainfall are readily available for most metropolitan regions. More importantly in most regions, the changing water level of streams in developing areas is continuously measured by gauging stations located at regular intervals. For each gauging station, hydrologists can construct relatively accurate hydrographs, which describe the amount of water flow (called "discharge") at the point of the gauging station.[5] From these water level measurements and from topographic maps of a given landscape, floodplain contour lines of a given recorded flood can be delineated. The accuracy of these flood contour lines is directly dependent upon the number of gauging stations, the length of the period for which these records have been kept, and the accuracy of topographic survey maps. When stream stage measurements are available for several decades and at frequent intervals, and when detailed topographic maps of approximately one-foot contour intervals are available, a hydrologist can predict flood probability lines with a high degree of accuracy. Several computerized mathematical models have been developed to determine flood probability using these data.[6] Figure 25 shows the application of a computerized flood hazard assessment technique. Accurate assessment of flood hazard,

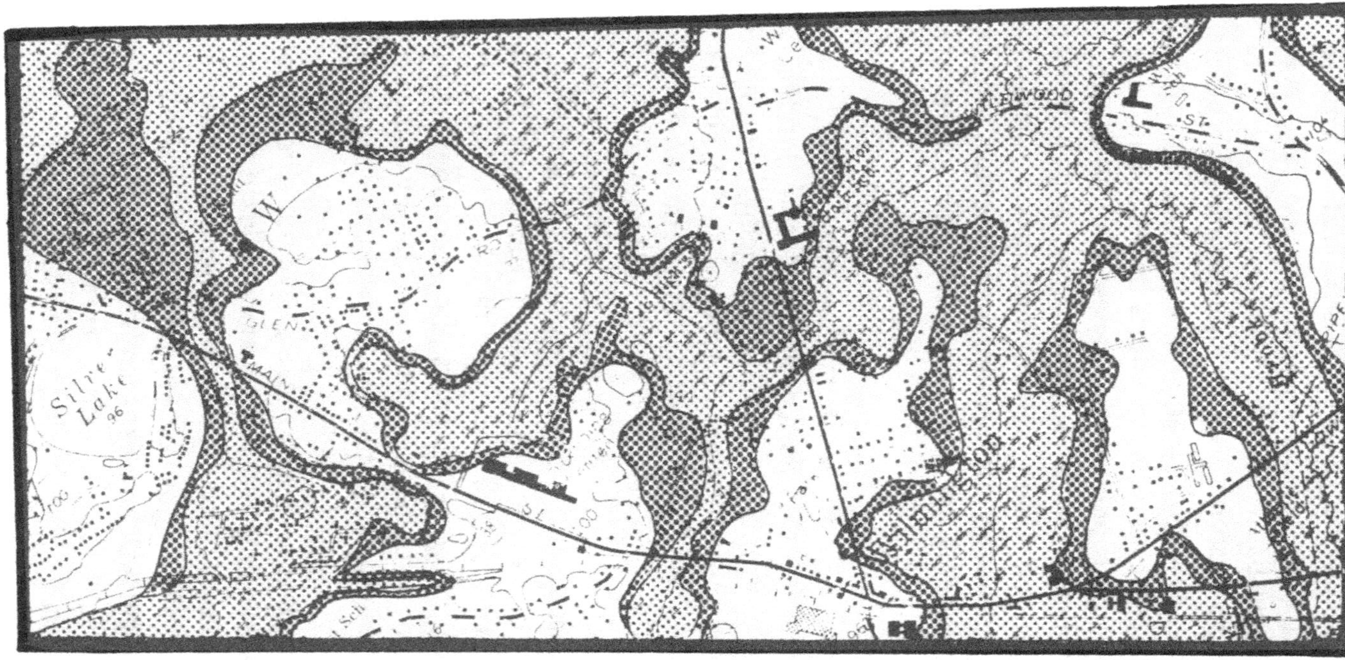

FIGURE 25. A comparison of the flood hazard assessment results when applied to a community subject to heavy metropolitan growth pressures from 1952 (lighter tone) to 1971 (darker tone). This process was applied to Wilmington, Massachusetts, in 1952 and 1971. An assessment of floodplain extent and land use types during this twenty-year period indicates the correlation of increased surface impermeability and increased floodplain size. In addition, as floodplain size grew, land uses that were free from flood hazard in 1952 became subject to that hazard probability by 1971, indicating the dynamic nature of the floodplain. To show this apparent floodplain change clearly, the figure represents only a small portion of the town of Wilmington.

The assessment process was developed by Dr. Donald Doehring and Susan Cole, environmental geologists of the University of Massachusetts landscape research group. The process evaluates the effects of urbanization on increasing the flood hazard over the twenty-year period. It also identifies those areas in which maximum economic flood loss occurs.

however, is an expensive process.

Because floodplain sizes change owing to urbanization, a major research question remains: how can we determine the flood level probabilities of a river basin that in the future may be fully developed at a metropolitan density? Planners need this type of information if the preventive planning approach is to be successful. Currently, several research efforts on this point have been undertaken in metropolitan landscapes. Remote sensing data provide information on land use change, and surficial geologic maps and soil data provide information on soil permeability. With this added information, the impact of various land use options on flooding will soon be predictable for differing types of terrain.[7]

Landslides: Mass Wasting. In most metropolitan areas, the hazard from landslides is less important than that from flooding, simply because most metropolitan regions have been developed on relatively flat landscapes. Certain flat landforms, such as alluvial fans, can be subject to severe "mass wasting" (as the movement of large amounts of earth is generically known.) However, most landslides usually occur on steep slopes. Planners also have developed norms that exclude from development those slopes that are 25 percent or steeper.[8] (A 45° angle represents a 100 percent slope: for every unit of horizontal distance, there is an equal unit of vertical distance.) Planners also recommend that slopes over 15 percent be developed at a lower density and with special care in regard to surface alteration and existing vegetative cover.

These present planning norms, however, have not eliminated the risk from mass wasting. At least five other variables in addition to slope should be considered in the assessment of landslide potential. These are soil composition, including particle size and range, surficial geologic structure, groundwater and soil moisture condition, climatic conditions in respect to rainfall distribution and intensity, and existing man-made stresses such as roads and buildings, which may affect sliding on a given site.[9] Environmental geologists and engineers with expertise in soil mechanics usually apply two techniques to determine the significance of these variables: on-site inspections (leaning gravestones in a cemetery, for example, indicate slow sliding) and subsurface explorations with boring tools and other devices. Geological maps, soil maps, and climatic data are also analyzed. Careful evaluation of these data can provide rough estimates of landslide potential.[10]

More recently, environmental geologists have moved beyond site-specific landslide probability assessment. Major landslide-prone regions, such as the Palos Verdes Hills in Los Angeles County, are being assessed and mapped to indicate relative landslide potential (see Figure 10). Planners can then use these to guide development away from the most hazardous areas.

Earthquakes. The significance of earthquakes for metropolitan regions was suggested in Chapter 2. Some seismic risk exists everywhere in the United States, with the exception of the lower portions of Texas, Louisiana, and Florida. Geologists estimate that major destructive earthquakes may occur in several heavily populated areas of the United States (shown as Zone 3 classifications in Figure 11).

Most earthquake-related research deals with developing techniques for designing buildings that can better withstand earthquakes[11] and warning devices that can predict potential earthquakes early enough to permit population evacuation. It would be simpler and safer to curb development where major destructive earthquakes are most likely to occur. Unfortunately, planners and decision makers have largely ignored geologists' warnings. The hazard of earthquakes seems to be less a problem of assessment than of communication.

HUMAN-CAUSED HAZARDS

Urban concentrations in the past often brought about polluted water supplies, but in developed countries, advancements in water resource and sanitary planning and in water and waste treatment have substantially reduced the health hazard from water pollution. Air pollution and unwanted noise, however, are still significant hazards of the metropolitan landscape, contributing to the exodus of many residents from central cities. As long ago as the fifteenth century, wealthy Italians began to build villas in the countryside, having rediscovered, in Newton's words, "the sweetness and freedom of the open air."[12] Louis XIV moved from Paris to Versailles for similar reasons during the seventeenth century. The contemporary separation of residential areas from commercial and other uses also reflects this syndrome.

Until recently, suburbia has provided a quieter and cleaner environment for many people. However, the continued expansion of suburban development and mushrooming traffic volumes have brought air and noise problems to most areas of the metropolis.

Air Pollution. The hazard potential of air pollution is significant on the global, regional, and local scale.[13] On the global level, the volume of pollutants produced today may eventually cause climatic changes that endanger future populations. The harm at the regional and metropolitan level is better understood, and it is at this level that planning activities have been the most significant. Evidence linking metropolitan area–wide air pollution to human illness and death is conclusive. Environmental pollutants such as carbon monoxide, oxides of sulphur and nitrogen, and photochemical oxidants are direct or contributing causes of nearly a dozen chronic diseases such as allergic asthma, cancer, and emphysema. Industrialized cities and regions have experienced dramatic episodes resulting in death or illness to thousands of residents. One of the most tragic episodes occurred in London in 1952, where approximately 4,000 deaths were linked to air pollution.[14]

Air pollution has had deleterious effects on plants and animals and has even damaged inert materials such as paint, building stone, and concrete.[15] A recent report claimed that in the United States the annual economic loss of inert materials from air pollution is about $104 billion.[16] Finally, the noxious odors and vapors are unpleasant aesthetically.

The multifaceted problem of air pollution has been studied by many scientists, including climatologists, chemists, physicists, biologists, and engineers. Climatologists and chemists have developed an impressive understanding of the geographical aspects of regional pollutants.[17] They have found that, among other factors, air flow, topography, and geographic location greatly influence the ability of pollutants to disperse in the atmosphere. Consequently, certain regions are more prone to pollution than others. Along the southern California coast, for example, thermal inversions (which limit the vertical mixing of air) and low winds (which limit its lateral movement) are present nearly 90 percent of the time during summer months.[18] From the point of view of air pollution hazard, the Los Angeles metropolis is one of the worst locations in the world for large-scale urbanization.

Air pollution assessment techniques at the regional level are well developed. The simulation models designed at the Argonne National Laboratory in the United States are representative of the current assessment and prediction capability. These quantitative, computerized models consider various factors (such as population growth and spatial allocation of pollution sources) for a spectrum of "criteria" pollutants (such as carbon monoxide, sulphur, nitrogen, hydrocarbons, and particulate matter) in making projections of regional air pollution conditions.[19] Models such as these suggest that lower-density development reduces air pollution potential. Large open space buffer zones combined with decreases in travel time are additional planning devices for air pollution control.

The third level of assessment addresses local air pollution problems. At this level, studies are designed to estimate the effects of various land uses on the air quality of adjacent land uses. They assess, for instance, the effect of a heavily traveled highway on nearby housing. Such estimates of air quality are being designed to provide planners with standards for the location of buffer strips between various land uses. Figure 26 shows the result of an air pollution assessment technique designed to estimate the effects of adjacent land uses in Burlington, Massachusetts.

Noise Pollution. Noise pollution, unlike air pollution, has not produced dramatic episodes of death and widespread illness. Nonetheless, noise has been shown to be harmful to people in several ways. Scientists note three common biological effects of noise. First, it affects the auditory system: prolonged exposure to noise can result in significant and permanent hearing losses.[20] Second, at extreme levels, noise can cause physiological effects on other parts of the human organism such as the digestive tract. Finally, noise is associated with psychological disorders and stress.[21]

Research on the problem of noise is taking place at three levels by three relatively distinct groups of scientists and planners. One of the earliest scientific groups to study noise pollution included biologists, physicians, and psychologists, who studied primarily the possible harm to human health, both physical and psychological. Much of their research was directed at noise in the workplace and in other noisy places such as construction sites and at the problem of hearing loss in particular. The effects of noise on the nonauditory system and the psychological state, however, have been less well researched. Nevertheless, a substantial number of research findings indicate that this kind of harm may be significant.[22]

The second group studying noise includes physicists and various kinds of engineers. These scientists have designed instruments to measure the characteristics of environmental sound. These measurements provide quantitative values of noise pollution that can be correlated with health conditions. Acoustical engineers and physicists are also responsible for the development of various mechanical noise reduction devices,[23] and they have analyzed the attenuation of noise as it travels from a source through the

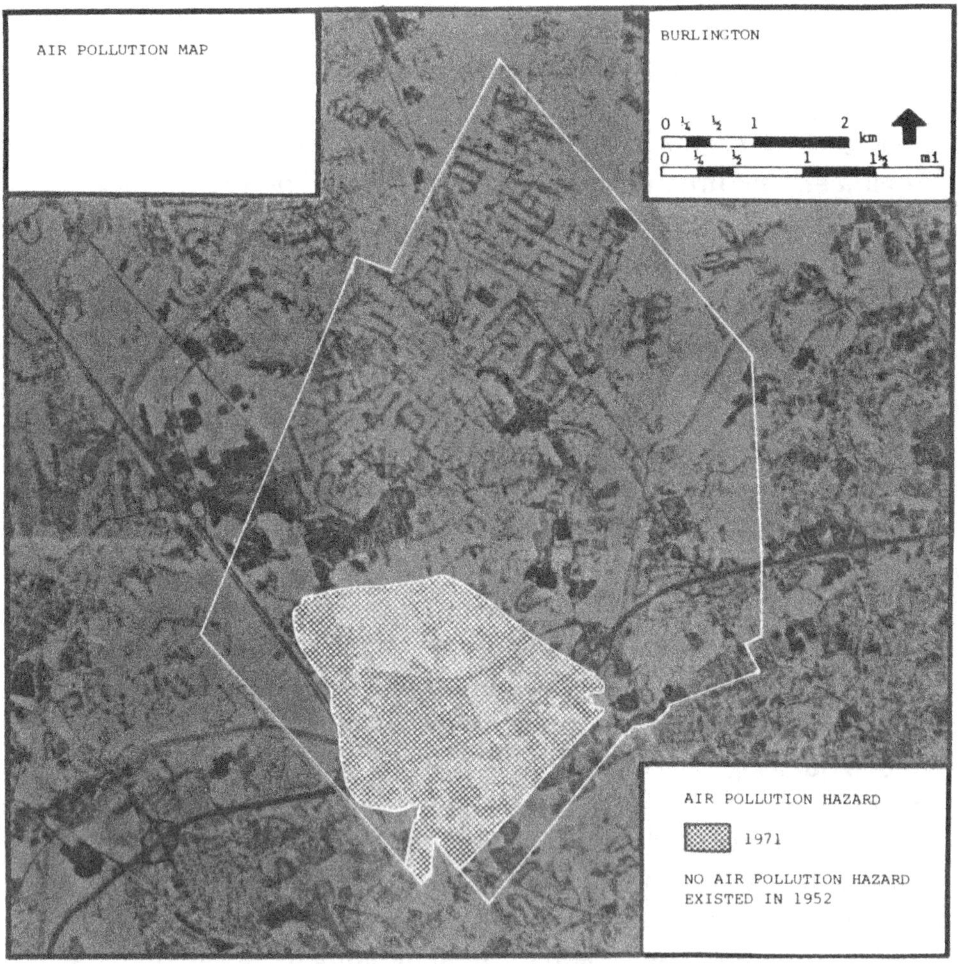

FIGURE 26. A comparison of the air pollution assessment results when applied to a community subject to heavy metropolitan growth pressures from 1952 to 1971. This process (on the third level of assessment) assessed land use contribution from effects of sulfur dioxide as a surrogate measure of general air pollution conditions. As may be seen where no air pollution hazard existed in 1952, a moderate potential hazard had developed by 1971. This hazard was caused by the proximate location of a large shopping center and industrialized development at the interchange of three superhighways.

The assessment process was developed by Victor Fahrer, environmental engineer of the University of Massachusetts landscape research group.

atmosphere and the landscape. This latter aspect of their study is especially pertinent to the establishment of environmental planning norms.

The third group that has investigated noise includes traffic engineers and urban and landscape planners. This group assesses noise for the purpose of land use planning, especially in the area of industrial use, highways, and airports.[24] Their primary objective is to develop planning norms that, if implemented, would minimize the effect of a noisy land use (such as a highway) on adjacent noise-sensitive land uses (such as a residential neighborhood). Because the effects of noise are spatially limited, noise pollution can be controlled more easily than air pollution.

The generalized assessment of noise is a new approach that has not yet been proved. It is based on the notion that particular land uses can be assigned a characteristic, typical ambient noise level. These levels are interpreted from the large number of site-specific measurements done by engineers and physicists. The distribution of noise levels throughout the metropolitan landscape, or any part of it, can be estimated by using this sort of generalized assessment technique. Figure 27 is the result of the application of such a technique.

Incompatible land uses can be modified to improve ambient sound levels. For new developments, appropriate land use selection can be made, and sufficient distance can be maintained between noise-sensitive and noise-generating uses. The distance needed between uses for desired noise attenuation is a function of several parameters, such as the height and density of vegetative cover and the height and thickness of man-made barriers. Table 1, developed by Caswell, estimates the distances planners must be aware of in order to maintain noise at desired levels.

The combined assessment of all major hazards discussed in this chapter is even more important than individual hazard assessments. Noise and localized air pollution often occur together. The distance needed to attenuate noise is often sufficient also to disperse localized air pollution caused by such land uses as highways. Floodplains, when protected from development, can

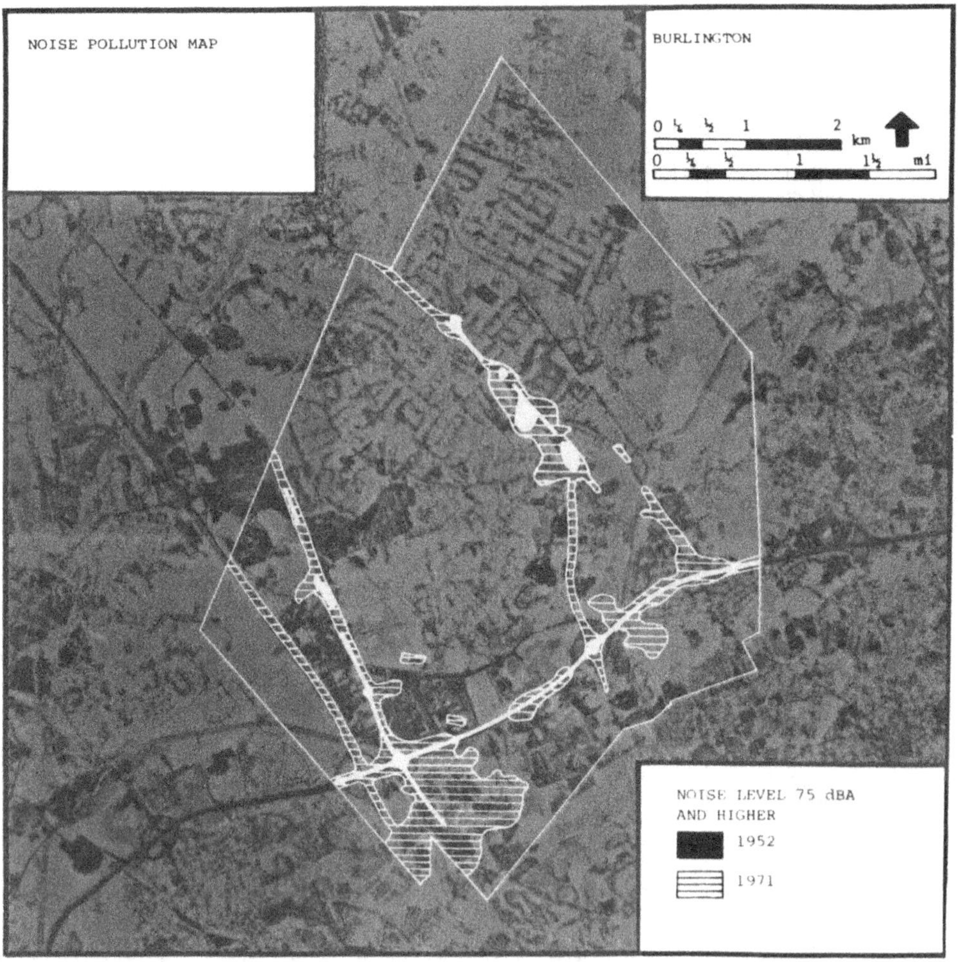

FIGURE 27. A comparison of the noise pollution hazard results when applied to a community subject to heavy metropolitan growth pressures from 1952 to 1971. The contour map shown indicates the amount of noise pollution effect and increase over the twenty-year period of urbanization. Compared to other hazards, the effects are relatively insignificant and are highly localized at major traffic arteries. The suburban noise problem could be solved by on-site design solutions, such as setbacks or buffers.

The assessment process was developed by Stephanie Caswell, resource specialist planner, and Dr. Karl Jakus, mechanical engineer of the University of Massachusetts landscape research group. The process evaluates the noise pollution effect caused by various land use types.

TABLE 1
Source-Receiver Distances

Source-receiver distances required to produce prescribed amounts of attenuation for eight alternative transmission path types (in feet), where dBA = frequency-weighted decibles and h_1 = that height of a barrier that is actually interrupting the sound traveling from a source to a receiver.

Total Attenuation (in dBA; *re* 0.0002 microbar)	TRANSMISSION PATH TYPE Distance Only	Agricultural Land or Grass	Reverting Field	Forest	Very Dense Forest	Barrier (h_1 = 5')	Barrier (h_1 = 10')	Barrier (h_1 = 15')
5	100	80	70	60	50	0	0	0
10	250	150	120	90	80	100	0	0
15	700	300	200	150	130	250	100	0
20	1600	600	300	250	200	700	250	100
25	2600	1000	500	350	300	1600	700	250
30	3800	1700	750	600	450	2600	1600	700
35	5000	2500	1000	800	600	3800	2600	1600
40	6500	3500	1300	1000	800	5000	3800	2600

Source: This table was adapted from the work of Stephanie Caswell, resource specialist of the University of Massachusetts landscape research group.

also be very useful buffer zones between incompatible land uses. Similarly, certain special resource value areas such as highly productive agricultural lands can be used as buffer zones. The more we know about resource values and hazard potentials, the better the ultimate land use decisions we can make.

NOTES

1. I. B. R. Kates and R. Snead, *The Human Ecology of Coastal Flood Hazard in Megalopolis*, University of Chicago, Department of Geography, Research Paper 115 (Chicago, Ill., 1969).
2. T. F. Saarinen, *Perception of the Drought Hazard on the Great Plains*, University of Chicago, Department of Geography, Research Paper 106 (Chicago, Ill., 1966).
3. L. B. Leopold, *Water: A Primer* (San Francisco: W. H. Freeman and Co., 1974), pp. 114-116.
4. P. M. Felton and H. W. Lull, "Suburban Hydrology Can Improve Watershed Conditions," *Public Works* 94, no. 1 (January 1963).
5. Leopold, *Water*, pp. 37-57.
6. S. G. Cole, D. O. Doehring, and J. Gy. Fabos, "Assessment of Flood Hazard Increases Due to Urbanization in the Greater Boston Area," *Proceedings of the Geologic Society of America* (Boulder, Colo.) 5, no. 1 (January 1974).
7. M. E. Smith, D. O. Doehring, and J. Gy. Fabos, "Process-Response Modeling of Flood Hazards in Twenty-Eight New England Basins," ibid., vol. 7, no. 1 (January 1975).
8. I. L. McHarg, *Design with Nature* (Garden City, N.Y.: The Natural History Press, 1969), p. 87.
9. P. T. Flawn, *Environmental Geology* (New York: Harper and Row, 1970), pp. 33-39; D. W. Way, *Terrain Analysis* (Stroudsburg, Pa.: Dowden, Hutchinson and Ross, 1973), pp. 23-31.
10. Flawn, *Environmental Geology*, pp. 38-39.
11. H. J. Lagorio and K. V. Steinbrugge, "Programming Earthquakes," *Progressive Architecture*, April 1974, pp. 62-67.
12. N. T. Newton, *Design on the Land: The Development of Landscape Architecture* (Cambridge, Mass.: The Belknap Press of Harvard University Press, 1971), p. 59.
13. R. A. Bryson, "All Other Factors Being Constant . . . —Theories of

Global Climatic Change," in *Man's Impact on Environment,* ed. T. R. Detwyler (New York: McGraw-Hill, 1971) pp. 167-174.

14. A. Stern, *Fundamentals of Air Pollution* (New York: Academic Press, 1973), pp. 127-137.

15. Ibid., pp. 112-124.

16. Ibid., p. 99.

17. P. A. Leighton, "Geographical Aspects of Air Pollution," in Detwyler, *Man's Impact on Environment,* pp. 113-130.

18. Ibid., p. 116.

19. E. J. Croke, "An Evaluation of the Impact of Land Use on Environmental Quality," in *Environment: A New Focus for Land-Use Planning,* ed. M. McAllister (Washington, D.C.: National Science Foundation, 1973).

20. A. Glorig, "Audiometric Testing in Industry," in *Handbook of Noise Control,* ed. C. M. Harris (New York: McGraw-Hill, 1975), pp. 5-1–5-22; J. Stataloff, L. Vassalo, and H. Menduke, "Temporary and Permanent Hearing Loss," *Archives of Environmental Health* 10 (1965):67-70.

21. W. H. Techner, E. Arees, and R. Reilly, "Noise and Human Performance: A Psychological Approach," *Ergonomics* 6 (1963):83-97; A. Cohen, "Effects of Noise on Psychological State," *Noise as a Public Health Hazard,* ASHA Report no. 4, eds. W. D. Ward and J. E. Ericke, (Washington, D.C.: American Speech and Hearing Association, 1969), pp. 74-88.

22. Techner, Arees, and Reilly, "Noise and Human Performance."

23. C. M. Harris, *Handbook of Noise Control* (New York: McGraw-Hill, 1957).

24. D. C. Colony, "Estimating Traffic Noise Levels and Acceptability for Freeway Design," *Highway Research Record,* no. 305 (1970), pp. 80-87; E. Guild, J. N. Cole, H. E. von Gierke, W. J. Galloway, and A. C. Pietrasanta, "Land Use Planning with Respect to Aircraft Noise: Discussion of a New Procedure," *Aerospace Medicine* 35, no. 8 (1964):719-723.

SUGGESTED READINGS

Books

Bernek, L., ed. *Noise Reduction.* New York: McGraw-Hill, 1960.

Detwyler, T. R. *Man's Impact on the Environment.* New York: McGraw-Hill, 1971.

Detwyler, T. R., and Marcus, J. *Urbanization and the Environment.* Belmont, Calif.: Duxbury Press, 1972.

Douglas, D. G., and Stewart, J. R., eds. *The Vanishing Landscape: A Collection of Critical Essays on Pollution and Environmental Control.* Skokie, Ill.: National Textbook Co., 1970.

Esposito, J. C. *Vanishing Air: The Ralph Nader Study Group on Air Pollution.* New York: Grossman Publishers, 1970.

Harris, C. M., ed. *Handbook of Noise Control.* New York: McGraw-Hill, 1957.

Hegecik, G. H. *Decision Making in Air Pollution Control.* New York: Praeger, 1970.

Herfindahl, O. C., and Knesse, A. V. *Quality of the Environment.* Baltimore: Johns Hopkins Press for Resources for the Future, 1965.

Hodgson, J. H. *Earthquakes and Earth Structure.* Englewood Cliffs, N.J.: Prentice-Hall, 1964.

Hor, J. *Air Pollution.* Pt. 1. New York: Marcel Delker, 1972.

Hoyt, W. G., and Langbein, W. B. *Floods.* Princeton, N.J.: Princeton University Press, 1955.

Knesse, A. V.; Rolpe, S. E.; and Harned, J. W. *Managing for the Environment: International Economic Cooperation for Pollution Control.* New York: Praeger, 1971.

Legget, R. H. *Cities and Geology.* New York: McGraw-Hill, 1973.

Leopold, L. *Water, A Primer.* New York: D. H. Freeman, 1974.

Mamantov, G. and Shulte, W. D., eds. *Determination of Air Quality.* New York: Plenum Press, 1972.

McKenzie, G. D. and Utgard, R. O. *Man and His Physical Environment: Readings in Environmental Geology.* Minneapolis: Burgess Press Publishing Co., 1972.

Newmark, Nathan, and Rosenblueth, E. *Fundamentals of Earthquake Engineering.* Englewood Cliffs, N.J.: Prentice-Hall, 1971.

Stern, A., ed. *Air Pollution.* Vols. 2-3. New York: Academic Press, 1968.

Tank, R. W. *Focus on Environmental Geology.* New York: Oxford University Press, 1973.

Turk, A., and Wittes, J. T. *Ecology, Pollution, Environment.* Philadelphia: Saunders, 1972.

Wang, J. Y.; Hemmer, W. B.; and Frederick, T. B. *Exploring Man's Environment.* Palo Alto, Calif.: Field Education Publications, 1973.

Periodicals

Pollution:

International Journal of Air Pollution. Journal of the Air Pollution Control

Institute, Air Pollution Control Association, Pittsburgh, Pa.

Earthquakes:

Abstract Journal in Earthquake Engineering. Earthquake Engineering Research Center, University of California, Berkeley, Calif.

Earthquake Information Bulletin. National Oceanic and Atmospheric Administration, Office of Public Affairs, Rockville, Md.

Journal of Earthquake Engineering and Structural Dynamics. International Association of Earthquake Engineers, Sussex, England.

Seismology Society of America Bulletins. Seismology Society of America Berkeley, Calif.

Floods:

Water Resources Research. American Geophysical Union, Washington, D.C.

University of Chicago, Department of Geography, research papers. Chicago, Illinois.

USGS Water Supply Papers and USGS Open File Reports, USGS, Reston, Va.

Air and Noise Hazards:

Archives of Environmental Health. American Academy of Occupational Medicine, Chicago, Ill.

Journal of the Acoustical Society of America. American Institute of Physics, New York.

Proceedings of the Congress on Environmental Health.

7 ASSESSMENT OF DEVELOPMENT SUITABILITY

The previous two chapters dealt with assessment procedures that are aimed at identifying areas where urban development is least appropriate. In the case of special-value landscape resources, development restrictions are suggested for those areas in which a valuable resource (or resources) is found. Similarly, hazard assessment identifies land where development would be jeopardized by natural or human-caused environmental hazards. The purpose of development, however, is to search out areas and sites that provide the optimal conditions for various uses—in other words, the areas and sites where development is *most* appropriate. Of course, many parcels of land will have attributes that render them simultaneously appropriate for development and worthy of protection from development. This often occurs in floodplains, for instance, where the physical, climatic, and visual constraints on development are minimal. This land is also likely to possess a high agricultural productivity value and be susceptible to flooding. It is the highlighting of such inherent conflicts that makes development suitability assessment such a potentially useful tool for land use planners. When applied in conjunction with resource and hazard assessment, it provides information for two types of decisions: (1) resource and hazard areas that are likely to be subject to the greatest development pressures can be reorganized; and (2) "trade-off" decisions regarding the priorities of alternative uses are made easier because what is likely to be gained and lost in any given decision can be assessed.

Systematic procedures for assessing development suitability are a relatively recent innovation. This is not to say that aspects of site or landscape suitability for various uses were not individually considered in the past. The designers of the Italian villas of the Renaissance understood the microclimatic and visual values of the hilltops where they placed their elegant houses and gardens. Similarly, farmers traditionally took into account the physical and microclimatic characteristics of their various parcels of land when deciding where to plant corn, grapes, or cereal grains.

Many of the new developments in rapidly growing metropolitan areas, however, are built in locations where the worst microclimatic conditions prevail or where the land is physically least suited to development. As technological developments have enabled builders to overcome natural land use constraints, the inherent suitability of the land has increasingly been ignored. Nevertheless, although an individual constraint may be negligible, the combined constraints of several variables often prove quite costly (in both dollars and energy consumption) and often give rise to undesirable, cumulative side effects. An awareness of this has provided an impetus in the past decade to improve the techniques of suitability assessment.

Most of the assessment techniques that have recently been developed are concerned with three facets of developent suitability: physical, climatic, and visual. The physical development suitability is a function of several landscape variables, such as slope and depth to water table. These characteristics may affect the cost of a given development as well as the impact of that development on the surrounding landscape. Climatic development suitability is a function of the localized landscape characteristics that affect the microclimate of a given area. For example, forest vegetation can provide shelter from cold winds during the winter season, and south-facing slopes usually receive much more sun in the winter than northern slopes. Microclimatic conditions clearly influence the heating and cooling of buildings, in addition to contributing directly to human comfort. Visual development suitability, finally, is a measure of the level of general amenity on any given piece of land. Although the presence of very high quality visual/values in an area may suggest that it be protected or preserved from development, a view of moderately high quality will nearly always enhance the development suitability of an area. For years, developers and economists have realized that many people are willing to pay more for houses that have a scenic view.

DEVELOPMENT SUITABILITY TECHNIQUES

At this time, development suitability assessment processes are more an art than a science. Several of the available techniques come not from the technical literature but rather from planning and design reports. These techniques seem to fall into three general categories: (1) development suitability techniques for a specific use (or uses) on a particular site, (2) general development suitability (or "site-selection") models for a specific use, and (3) comprehensive suitability assessments of an area of public jurisidiction (such as a township or region) for all major categories of development.

Development suitability techniques for use on a particular site. This category contains the earliest suitability techniques. Designers and planners, especially landscape architects, have been hired by developers to analyze and evaluate the physical, climatic, and visual characteristics of a site. Most often, decisions on the type of development and its density have been made before these professionals have been hired. For instance, a developer might plan to locate 500 townhouse units and 300 single-family houses on a 250-acre (100-hectare) site. He or she might also plan to set aside a passive recreation area for the community. The designers he or she hires might proceed as follows. First, physical, climatic, and visual characteristics of the site are mapped on individual analysis maps. These are then combined in a composite map, which represents the assessed values of each portion of the site for various uses (see Figure 28). The areas with drier soils and good views are set aside for housing. Wetlands and drainage areas are set aside for passive recreation. Conflicts sometimes arise between developers and designers, e.g., when this assessment finds a site to be ideally suited for fewer units than the developer had planned. In most development, however, this problem does not arise, because the development plans are implemented without the bother of a detailed site analysis and evaluation in the first place.

Development Suitability Models for a Specific Use or Uses. Models of this type have been designed by several planners and designers during the past decade. Site-selection models for various recreation uses, such as camping or boating, are among the most common and are usually prepared by planning or various advisory agencies. But they do not enjoy widespread publicity, either in books or journals. Among the studies prepared by planning agencies is the voluminous *Outdoor Recreation Planning in Michigan by a Systems Approach.* This report includes several detailed processes for the selection of the most appropriate sites for various recreational uses. For instance, all the lakes in the state of Michigan are ranked in terms of their attraction for boating on the basis of size, depth, water quality, surrounding landscape quality, and other characteristics.[1]

Advisory agencies in the United States have also developed processes for the site selection of recreational uses. The New Hampshire Cooperative Extension Service, for example, has developed a process for evaluating campground sites, a process in which water, topography, soil, vegetation, and visual quality are among the factors evaluated.[2] Similarly, the United States Soil Conservation Service has developed a systematic approach for assessing twelve standard categories of outdoor recreation areas,[3] an approach that can be used either by state and local planning agencies or by private recreation developers.

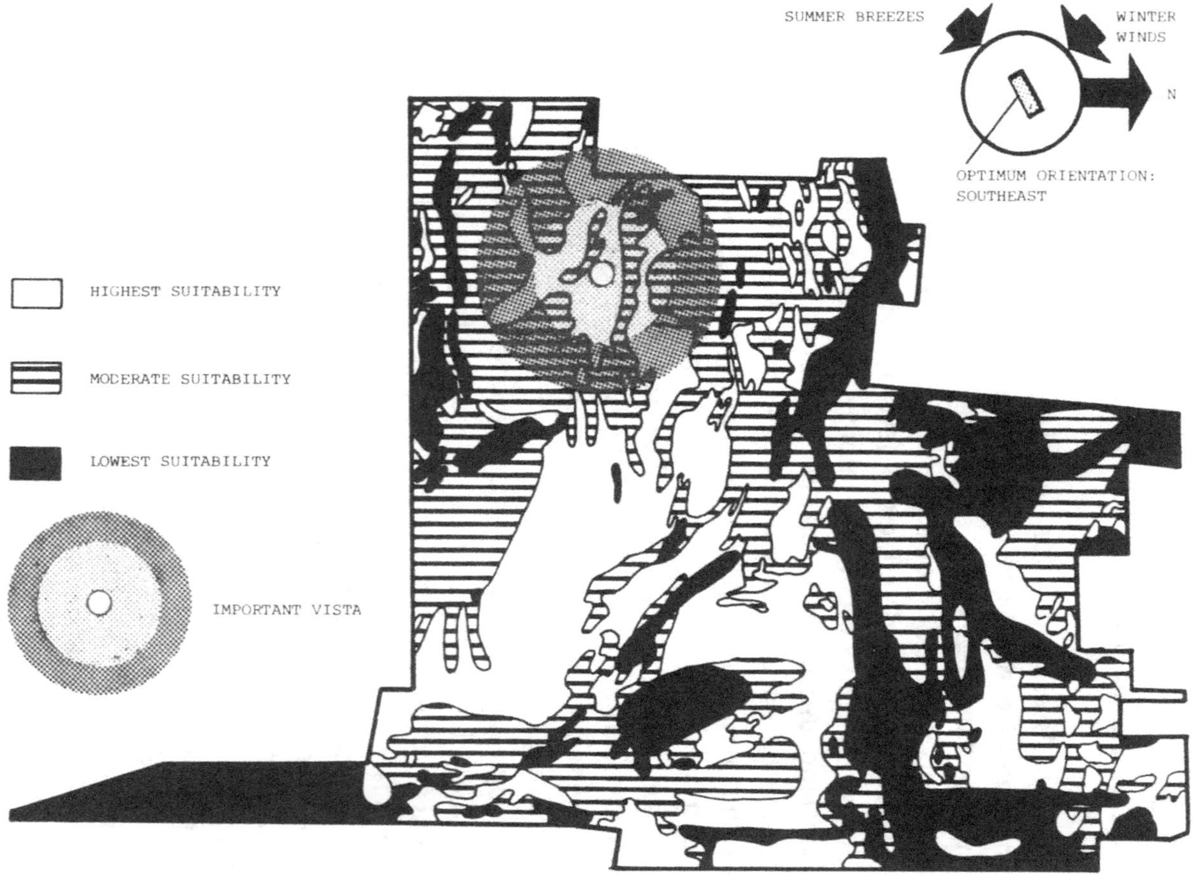

FIGURE 28. A composite site assessment map for Manchester site.

Notably absent from this group of techniques are development suitability models for housing, industrial, or commercial uses. Unfortunately, owing to this lack of environmental models, developers have depended on economic models that assess market potentials and locational factors.

Suitability Assessments for All Major Development Types. Comprehensive suitability assessments represent the latest and most important step in development suitability planning. Such assessments of a region or township could help minimize many unwanted negative side effects of developments. In addition, they could decrease its costs while improving human comfort. Most public land use decision makers, however, make incremental decisions that concern only specific developments. When they do take a more comprehensive planning approach, they concentrate on long-range transportation, housing, economic development, education, or social issues to the exclusion of environmental concerns. Consequently, the land use patterns that many "master plans" generate seldom reflect the natural landscape resources of the community or region.

Although well-developed assessment techniques, which combine physical, climatic, and visual resource factors, are not yet in existence, some progress is beginning to be made in this area. General landscape planning processes such as those popularized by landscape architect Ian McHarg are used by some community and regional agencies.[4] The design and planning firm of Rahenkamp, Sacks, Wells, and Associates is vigorously promoting its "Impact Zoning System," which addresses many issues related to suitability.[5]

As for the several factors of development suitability, the assessment techniques for the physical factor have been developed the furthest. Because of the recent energy crisis, however, more and more attention is being paid to climatic assessment methods. At this point, the visual factor is the least understood. Nevertheless, most planners agree that the high-quality visual aspects of a landscape should be considered a contribution to development suitability.

PHYSICAL DEVELOPMENT SUITABILITY

Many studies of physical development suitability consider several development-related aspects of the surface of the earth. The most frequently cited variable is the depth to water table. A high water table presents certain constraints to development, which must be overcome by drainage devices, pumps, or special construction techniques. A second common variable is the depth to bedrock. When solid, hard bedrock is close to the surface of the ground, development costs can increase sharply. Excavation of bedrock may require the use of explosives and can be very expensive. It may also contribute to unwanted construction side effects, such as noise and dust pollution. A third frequently used variable is slope. The steeper the slope of the ground, the more difficult the construction usually is. Steep slopes also increase the length of access roads and can increase erosion problems both during and after construction.

Other less significant variables that are sometimes evaluated include: (1) soil drainage characteristics, (2) soil-bearing capacity (sandy soils can support heavier structures, peat soils in marshy areas cannot), (3) stoniness (large boulders may increase certain development costs), (4) erodibility (soils that erode easily add to development costs and cause undesirable siltation of natural drainage systems, and (5) topsoil (good topsoil can be set aside during initial site clearing and spread after construction to accelerate plant growth).

Many disciplines have an interest in the variables of the physical factor, but three are very important: soil science, environmental geology, and landscape architecture/planning. The first two disciplines are concerned with the detailed, scientific aspects of soil, surficial geology, and hydrology. Landscape architects/planners attempt to use interpreted information for the planning and design of development.

The geologist and soil scientist obtain their data primarily from fieldwork, although they occasionally prepare generalized maps from air photos. Soil and surficial geological maps at many scales have been prepared by public agencies in the United States for nearly a hundred years. Obviously, the smaller-scale maps are more general, and larger-scale maps are usually more detailed and specific. General soil or surficial geologic maps are used for preliminary planning. These are accurate to about fifty acres (twenty hectares).

More detailed maps may be accurate to about three acres (approximately one hectare). This detail is sufficient for land use planning on the meso-scale, such as planning for a community. For specific site design, additional, more detailed data are nearly always required.

During the past several decades, the governments of most developed countries have spent a great deal of money on the preparation of soil and surficial geologic maps and on interpretative maps that are useful for planning. The Massachusetts Soils Conservation Service, for example, has prepared detailed soil maps and several interpretative maps for most towns in the larger Boston metropolitan regions.[6] These interpretive maps were made for various purposes, for example, to estimate the percolation capacity of soils for on-site sewage disposal in housing developments without access to public sewer systems. General soil suitabilities for home sites, athletic fields, and roads have also been interpreted. These interpretive soil maps are widely used by planners and developers.

Environmental geologists have also prepared interpretive maps that are useful for the planning of fast-growing metropolitan regions. These maps are not yet as commonly used as soil studies, mainly because only a few regions have been interpreted for planning purposes. The value of interpretive geologic maps is that the information they provide about bedrock, water table, and drainage conditions is more accurate than that provided by soil maps. The soil scientist is interested primarily in the top five to six feet of the earth's surface. The surficial geologist goes significantly deeper.

These two sets of limitation maps are together sufficient for determining the development suitability of the physical factor. Landscape planners have worked with these scientists to improve the utility of interpretive maps. The major drawback in assessing the physical factor at this time is our lack of knowledge about explicit costs in overcoming any or all of the limitations discussed. Furthermore, the intangible or nonmonetary environmental costs are even less well defined. Much more work is needed to improve the present physical suitability assessment techniques for environmental planning. As an illustration of the present level of physical assessment techniques, Figure 29 shows the results of applying a development suitability process that evaluates each of the physical variables discussed above.

CLIMATIC DEVELOPMENT SUITABILITY

Regional climatic differences, such as those that characterize temperate or hot arid climatic zones, are well documented. Metropolitan regions usually do not lie in more than one of these general climatic zones. At the regional scale, therefore, climate is seldom an issue. Microclimatic variation among the different parts of a region, however, is often significant (many climatologists call this level of climatic assessment "topoclimatic"). This scale of climatic variation concerns us for three reasons. First, developments that are exposed to extreme temperatures, either hot or cold, require extra energy for heating or cooling. Second, those areas in which microclimatic effects are extreme are less comfortable to live in. Third, for certain uses such as airports and highways, adverse microclimatic conditions, such as fog "pockets," can significantly affect the safety of their operation.

To assess an area's microclimate, planners need information on several variables, including (1) orientation to the sun (in

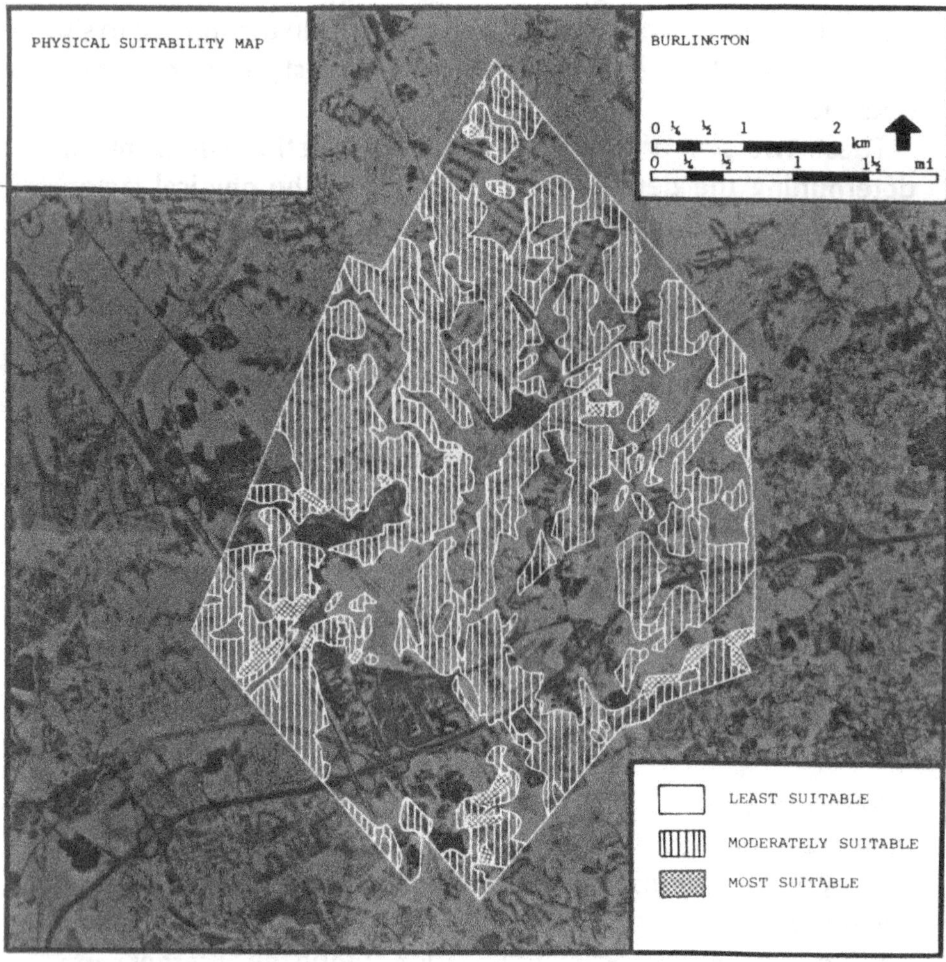

FIGURE 29. A comparison of the physical variable assessment results when applied to a community subject to heavy metropolitan growth from 1952 to 1971. Noticeable in the aerial photograph is a major highway in the southern portion of the town. This highway and four exits from it were located in an area where the soil conditions were generally unsuitable. The predictable result, as may be seen in the figure, was the generation of significant residential, industrial, and commercial development in environmentally unsuitable areas.

The assessment process was developed by Robert Reiter, landscape architect and member of the University of Massachusetts landscape research group. The process uses soil survey information developed by the USDA Soil Conservation service. Suitability factors analyzed include depth to water, depth to bedrock, slope, bearing capacity/stability, erodibility, topsoil, stoniness, and drainage. These were weighted in terms of their estimated importance in determining developmental suitability.

the northern hemisphere, slopes with southern orientations receive more radiation than northern slopes, especially in the winter when the sun is lower in the sky); (2) orientation to winds, (exposure to prevailing winter winds increases heat costs and decreases comfort, and exposure to summer winds moderates heat and increases comfort); (3) topographic features (these may shield winds or channel their direction); (4) vegetation, which can protect development from winter winds; and (5) water bodies (large lakes or oceans can have a climatic influence for several miles inland).

Although scientists agree that these variables are significant, sufficient quantitative data are not available to specify the difference between two microclimatic areas in regard to changes in heating or cooling costs and comfort. Only general energy cost-related information is available. We know, for instance, that space heating accounts for 42 percent of residential energy use in the United States.[7] However, quantitative information on the difference between the energy needs of the same type of development on a north slope versus a south slope, with and without vegetation, is not available.

The number of disciplines interested in microclimatic assessment has increased recently. A little over a decade ago, only a few lonely designers and climatologists wrote about microclimatic considerations for planning and design.[8] With the recent energy crisis, though, many scientists from physics, engineering, geography, and other fields have joined in the study of microclimatic differences. Computerized mathematical models are now being built to determine and map the amount of solar radiation received by different sites. Useful results for planning and design, however, are only now becoming available.

Nonetheless, the microclimatic literature of the early 1960s has helped establish some planning and design norms. Many master plans show a sensitivity to the importance of primary winds, slope orientation, and the potential of vegetation buffers as windbreaks. Systematic microclimatic development suitability assessment, however, is still in the early stages of development. A landscape research group at the University of Massachusetts has attempted to design a microclimatic assessment model. The initial approach is presented in Figure 30.

VISUAL DEVELOPMENT SUITABILITY

Most techniques of visual assessment (see, e.g., Figure 24) have been concerned primarily with areas of such scenic importance that their protection from development is desired for long-range public benefits. However, scenic quality also enhances the amenity of urban development.

McKeever, in a discussion of commercial and business projects, states that "good views and pleasing outlook are great assets in the marketability of a development project."[9] A study of housing developments by Payne, an economist, demonstrated that the existence of trees in residential developments increased house and lot value by an average of 7 percent and in some cases, by as much as 15 percent.[10] In this context, then, there is clearly a measure of visual development suitability that will characterize any site and which should be assessed as a complement to the identification of spectacular landscapes for preservation purposes.

A sophisticated quantified process that evaluates the values of views and trees has not yet been developed, even though landscape architects consistently consider these variables on their analysis and composite assessment maps (see Figure 28). Some individual studies aimed at quantifying view quality are beginning to be carried out, however. For example, scientists of the U.S. Forest Service have designed a computerized model that can map the view areas of a landscape from topographic and vegetation data (Figure 31).[11]

The capacity of trees to act as visual screens is also under study at the present time. When development occurs on open, flat landscapes, it often appears intrusive, unless the architecture is

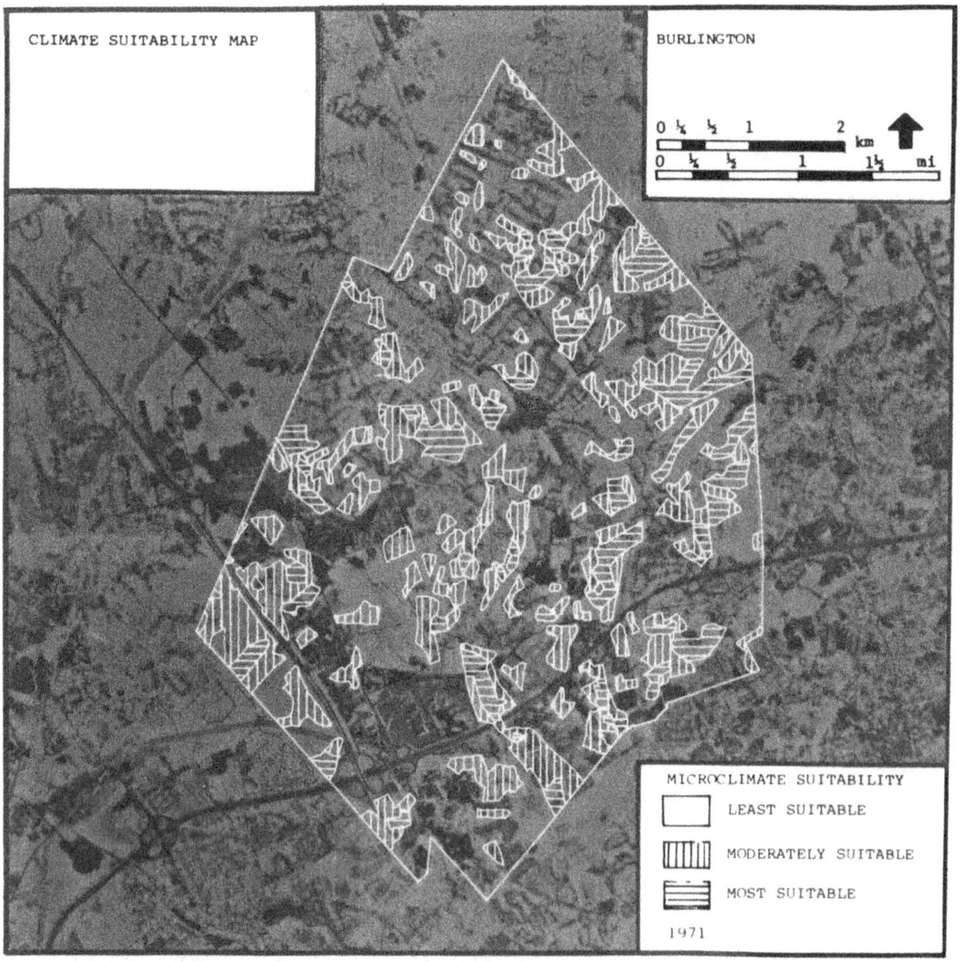

FIGURE 30. A comparison of the microclimatic assessment results when applied to a community subject to heavy metropolitan growth pressures from 1952 to 1971. There appears to be very little correlation between microclimatic suitability and the development pattern shown in the airphoto. Although microclimatic suitability may be significant in a topographically more valued landscape, it may be of little importance in the relatively flat landscape depicted here. Present indications are that site design strategies such as the location of shade trees or building orientation may be more significant in terms of microclimatic effects. More research is needed to substantiate this hypothesis.

The assessment process was developed by Robert Reiter, landscape architect and member of the University of Massachusetts landscape research group. The process evaluates solar and wind orientation, topographic features, and vegetation in estimating the degree of microclimatic suitability for development.

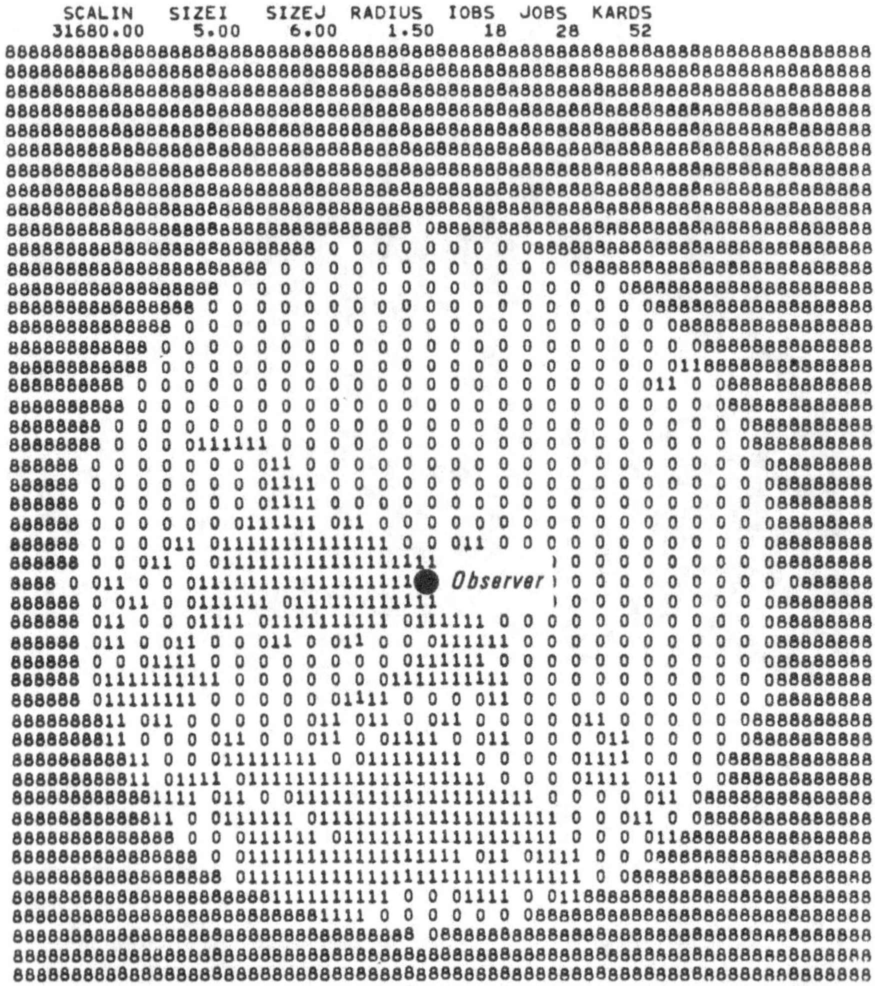

FIGURE 31. Illustrates the application of a computer program, which shows all areas that can be seen from the center of the circle.

The computer program was developed by Elliot Amidon and G. H. Elsner, members of the United States Forest Service research team, Berkeley, California, Pacific Southwest Forest and Range Experiment Station.

sensitively designed. Trees, however, can significantly ameliorate the intrusive effect of poor or mediocre development.[12] If the new metropolitan development of the North Atlantic megalopolitan region were to occur in forest lands, which cover 50 percent of the region, the visual impact of this development would be small.

In summary, the importance of the concept of development suitability should be reiterated. Each of the three factors reviewed has been found to be significant by scientists and planners. Although suitability assessment is presently less developed than special resource or hazard assessment, it is anticipated that during the next decade impressive advancements will occur in this area.

NOTES

1. J. Gy. Fabos, "An Analysis of Environmental Quality Ranking Systems," *Proceedings of Recreation Symposium,* USDA Forest Service (Syracuse, N.Y., 1971), p. 51.
2. Ibid.
3. Ibid.
4. I. L. McHarg, *Design with Nature* (Garden City, N.Y.: The Natural History Press, 1969).
5. "Impact Zoning," *Housing and Home,* 42, no. 2 (August 1972):58-67.
6. B. Isgur, *Status of Soil Conservation Service Program in Massachusetts* (USDA Soil Conservation Service, January 1975).
7. D. Myhra, "Let's Put an End to Energy Waste in Housing," *Planning,* August 1974, p. 17.
8. V. Olgyay, *Design with Climate: Bioclimatic Approach to Architectural Regionalism* (Princeton, N.J.: Princeton University Press, 1963); R. Geiger, *The Climate near the Ground* (Cambridge, Mass.: Harvard University Press, 1965).
9. I. R. McKeever, *Business Parks: Office Parks, Plazas and Centers* (Washington, D.C.: The Urban Land Institute, 1970).
10. B. R. Payne, "The Twenty-nine Tree Home Improvement

Plan," *The Metro Forest*, A Natural History Special Supplement, November 1973, pp. 74-75.

11. E. L. Amidon and G.H. Elsner, "Delineating Landscape View Areas: A Computer Approach," Pacific Southwest Forest and Range Experiment Station, USDA Forest Service, Research Note PSW-180, Berkeley, Calif., 1968.

12. P. Jacobs and D. Way, *Visual Analysis of Landscape Development* (Cambridge, Mass.: Department of Landscape Architecture, Graduate School of Design, Harvard University, 1969).

SUGGESTED READINGS

Books

Aronin, J. E. *Climate and Architecture.* New York: Reinhold, 1953.

Bartelli, L. J., et al., eds. *Soil Surveys and Land Use Planning.* Madison, Wis.: 1966.

Bates, R. L. *Geology of the Industrial Rocks and Minerals.* New York: Dover Publications, 1969.

Coates, D. R. *Environmental Geomorphology and Landscape Conservation.* Stroudsburg, Pa.: Dowden, Hutchinson, and Ross, 1972.

Detwyler, T. R., ed. *Man's Impact on the Environment.* New York: McGraw-Hill, 1971.

Flawn, P. T. *Environmental Geology.* New York: Harper and Row, 1970.

Geiger, R. *The Climate Near the Ground.* Cambridge, Mass.: Harvard University Press, 1961.

Gottman, J. *Megalopolis: The Urbanized Northeastern Seaboard of the United States.* Cambridge, Mass.: MIT Press, 1961.

Hackett, B., *Landscape Planning.* Newcastle-on-Tyne, England: Oriel Press, 1971.

Lynch, K. *Site Planning.* 2d ed. Cambridge, Mass.: MIT Press, 1972.

McBoyle, Geoffrey, ed. *Climate in Review.* Boston: Houghton Mifflin, 1973.

McCue, G. M. *Creating the Human Environment: A Report of the American Institute of Architects.* Urbana: University of Illinois, 1970.

McKeever, J. R. *The Community Builders Handbook.* Washington, D.C.: The Urban Land Institute, 1968.

Mather, J. R. *Climatology: Fundamentals and Applications.* New York: McGraw-Hill, 1974.
Olgyay, V. *Design with Climate: Bio-Climatic Approach to Architectural Regionalism.* Princeton, N.J.: Princeton University Press, 1963.
Steadman, P. *Energy Environment and Building.* Cambridge, Mass.: Harvard University Press, 1975.
Way, D. *Terrain Analysis.* Stroudsburg, Pa.: Dowden, Hutchinson, and Ross, 1973.

Periodicals

Land, General Physical Resources:
Journal of Wildlife Management. Soil Conservation Society Publications, Ankeney, Iowa.
Soil Science. Williams and Williams Co., Baltimore, Md.
Urban Land. Urban Land Institute, Washington, D.C.
USDA Soils Guides. U.S. Department of Agriculture, Washington, D.C.
Water Resources Research. "Effects of Construction on Sediment." American Geophysical Union, Washington, D.C.

Visual:
Landscape Architecture. American Society of Landscape Architects, McLean, Va.
Natural Environment. Natural Environment Research Council, Great Britain.

Climate:
Agricultural Meteorology. Elsevier Publishing Co., Amsterdam, Netherlands.
Climatological Data. U.S. Weather Bureau, Washington, D.C.
Weather. Royal Meteorologic Society, London, England.

8 ASSESSMENT OF HUMAN IMPACT ON THE ENVIRONMENT

The natural environment functions as a complex, interrelated system; when undisturbed by human activities, it maintains a balance between the forces of creation and the forces of destruction. This chapter deals with the methods that are available, first, to assess the degree of perturbation of the "natural balance" caused by human land use activities and, second, to assess the capacity of the natural environment to tolerate human land use activities without significant detriment to its regenerative capabilities. In both instances, the environment is considered as a system. This perspective contrasts with and complements the assessment of individual disaggregated landscape attributes discussed in the chapters on resources, hazards, and development suitability.

Technological growth in the past five decades has greatly increased our ability to intervene both wittingly and unwittingly in natural processes. The "spillover" effects on the environment of most of our activities, however, have not usually been perceived as matters for concern. As Marquis has commented, "When faced with the need to act on specific uncertainties, men have proceeded to do so without concerning themselves about the analysis and control of surprise repercussions."[1]

The analysis of "surprise repercussions" from land use activities must proceed from two points: an understanding of how the environment works and an understanding of how a given land use or pattern of uses affects that working. The science of ecology has provided a number of answers to these and other questions about environmental function. Only recently, however, has research begun to look into the dimensions of "environmental impact" of human activities. The rest of this chapter will discuss impact assessment techniques as they are currently developed and will then consider the progress that has been made toward assessing the inherent capacity of the environment to accommodate development.

ENVIRONMENTAL IMPACT ASSESSMENT

The public awareness that some of the things that we, as a society, had become accustomed to doing were having severe and sometimes irreversible impacts on the natural environment has been stimulated by several eloquent spokesmen—such as Rachel Carson, whose alarming report on pesticide pollution, *Silent Spring*, was published in 1962.[2] Many ecologists have themselves undertaken to expand the public's consciousness of environmental issues—such as Raymond Dasmann, senior ecologist of the International Union for Conservation of Nature, who has addressed the apparent dilemma between the environment and population growth.[3] Journalists and scientists have been joined in the effort to popularize the significance of environmental issues by a number of public officials as well. While secretary of the interior under Presidents Kennedy and Johnson, Stewart Udall published two provocative books on the conflict between human activities and the environment.[4]

The work of these writers and many others engendered a broadly based concern for environmental issues. In 1969 this concern resulted in Congress's articulation of a national policy toward the environment: "It is the continuing policy of the Federal government . . . to use all practicable means and measures

. . . in a manner calculated to foster and promote the general welfare, to create and maintain conditions under which man and nature can exist in productive harmony, and fulfill the social, economic, and other requirements of present and future generations of Americans."[5] One of the central features of the National Environmental Policy Act (NEPA) was a requirement that an "environmental impact" statement be included in every report on proposals for major federal actions that "significantly affect the quality of the human environment."[6] The effects of this requirement have been far-reaching. Perhaps no other governmental action has been so great an impetus to the field of environmental landscape assessment. By 1973, only four years after the passage of NEPA, some 4,000 mandated environmental impact statements had been prepared.[7] The demand for accurate and efficient impact assessment techniques and for personnel capable of carrying them out has stimulated the establishment of consulting firms who specialize in impact statement writing as well as of many similar departments in larger firms. The extension of the impact assessment idea to state-level projects has further accelerated these developments.[8]

As might be supposed, the quality of the various environmental impact statements varies enormously. Most of the assessment techniques involve the completion of a matrix in which existing environmental characteristics and conditions are listed along one axis and proposed actions that may have an environmental impact along the other axis. In the simpler techniques, the matrix is completed merely by entering "yes" or "no"for each combination of proposed action and existing condition, depending on whether an impact of some sort is anticipated. More sophisticated methods attempt to quantify both the significance and magnitude of the existing environmental characteristics, as well as the severity of the anticipated impact from each proposed action.[9] Some of these quantification efforts are based on well-established research findings (such as the deleterious effect on fish populations of increases in water temperature), but many are based on more subjective, intuitive estimates on the part of the evaluators.

At this writing, the validity of most environmental impact statements is less than ideal. But perhaps more importantly, they have failed to accomplish their lofty goal as set forth in the 1969 act: "to achieve a balance between population and resource use. . . for future generations."[10] One of the major reasons for this failure relates not to problems of validity, but rather to the fact that impact assessments are made only after a decision has been taken to build something.

A more useful approach would be to estimate the maximum number of people and the maximum intensity of uses that could be absorbed by a given region before the decision to undertake a project. This estimate is often referred to as the environmental "carrying capacity." With this kind of information, long-range, strategic land use planning could begin to supplant the current pattern of disjointed, incremental decisions that have to be taken each time another dam, power plant, or subdivision is proposed.

Progress toward the development of valid and useful methods for determining an area's environmental carrying capacity has been slow. The variables involved are extraordinarily complex, and the definition of conditions under which an ecosystem can no longer naturally renew itself is highly problematic. Nonetheless, several important conceptual steps toward this goal have been made.

Most research in this area, not surprisingly, has been undertaken by ecologists. At its inception, the science of ecology considered the environment from a holistic perspective. It then developed the notion of an ecosystem, a finite segment of the environment that functions as a more or less self-sustaining ecological community. Much effort has been focused on detailing the functional and biotic components of ecosystems. Only recently have ecologists returned to a consideration of the whole in terms of formal and mathematical models.[11] It is in this area that the most useful formulations for planning purposes have emerged.

The "compartmental" model developed by Eugene Odum, as suggested in Chapter 3, has considerable relevance for planning at the metropolitan level. By classifying inhabited regions into four functional "compartments"—productive, protection, nonvital (urban), and compromise—this model implies that an environmentally prudent land use allocation should be based on the ecological characteristics of the landscape. Odum proposed that the location, size, distribution, and intensity of land uses in each of the four compartments in any region should be inventoried using advanced remote sensing and geographic data manipulation techniques. Then, an application of sophisticated computerized simulation models would yield an indication of the dimensions of future urban growth in a region that would continually maintain a desired level of environmental quality.

Odum first published these thoughts in an article entitled "The Strategy of Ecosystem Development" in 1969.[12] Since this article was published, researchers have begun to explore the feasibility of implementing such a scheme. Although the results of these efforts are still incomplete, the prospect of success seems good.

NOTES

1. S. Marquis, "Ecosystems, Societies and Cities," *The American Behavioral Scientist,* July-August 1968, p. 13.
2. R. Carson, *The Silent Spring* (Boston: Houghton, Mifflin, 1962).
3. R. F. Dasmann, *Environmental Conservation* (New York: John Wiley and Sons, 1959).
4. S. L. Udall, *The Quiet Crisis* (New York: Avon Books, 1963); *1976: Agenda for Tomorrow* (New York: Harcourt, Brace and World, 1968).
5. B. C. Kross, "Preparation of an Environmental Impact Statement," *University of Colorado Law Review* 44 (1972-1973):82.
6. Ibid., p. 81.
7. R. H. Twiss, "Linking the EIS to the Planning Process," *Environmental Impact Assessment: Commentary and Guidelines* (Berkeley, Calif.: University of California Extension Service, 1974), p. 5.
8. R. W. Burchell and D. Listokin, *The Environmental Impact Handbook* (New Brunswick, N.J.: Center for Urban Policy Reserch,

Rutgers University, 1975), p. 7.

9. L. P. Leopold, F. E. Clarke, B. B. Handshaw, and J. R. Balsley, *A Procedure for Evaluating Environmental Impact,* Geological Survey Circular 645, U.S. Geological Survey (Washington, D.C., 1971).

10. Kross, "Preparation," p. 82.

11. C. J. Walters, "Systems Ecology: The Systems Approach and Mathematical Models in Ecology," in *Fundamentals of Ecology,* ed. E. P. Odum (Philadelphia: Saunders, 1971), p. 276.

12. E. P. Odum, "The Strategy of Ecosystem Development," *Science* 164 (April 1969).

SUGGESTED READINGS

Books

Bosselman, F. and Callies, D. *The Quiet Revolution in Land Use Control.* Prepared for the Council on Environmental Quality. Washington, D.C.: Government Printing Office, 1971.

Burchell, R. W., and Listokin, D. *The Environmental Impact Handbook.* Center for Urban Policy Research, Rutgers University. New Brunswick, N.J., 1975.

Isard, W. *Ecologic-Economic Analysis for Regional Development.* New York: Free Press, 1972.

Maddox, J. *The Doomsday Syndrome.* New York: McGraw-Hill, 1972.

Odum, E. *Fundamentals of Ecology.* 3rd ed. Philadelphia: Saunders, 1971.

Odum, H. T. *Environment, Power and Society.* New York: Wiley Interscience, 1971.

Pitton, R. B. and Goodale, T. L. *Environmental Impact Analysis: Philosophy and Methods.* Proceedings of the Conference on Environmental Impact Analysis, Green Bay, Wisconsin, January 4-5, 1972.

Twiss, R. H. *Linking the EIS to the Planning Process. Environmental Impact Assessment: Commentary and Guidelines,* U.C. Extension, Berkeley, Calif., 1974.

Van Dyne, M. *The Ecosystem Concept in Natural Resource Management.* New York: Academic Press, 1969.

Watt, K. E. *Ecology and Resource Management.* New York: McGraw-Hill, 1968.

___. *Systems Analysis in Ecology.* New York: Academic Press, 1966.

Periodicals

Congressional Record. U.S. Congress, Washington, D.C.

Environmental Law Reporter. Environmental Law Institute, Washington, D.C.

HUD "Handbook of Departmental Policies, Responsibilities and Procedures for Protection and Enhancement of E.Q." Ped., Register vol. 38, no. 137, Pt. 3, U.S. Government Printing Office, Washington, D.C., July 18, 1973.

Land and Water Review. University of Wyoming, Laramie, Wyo.

Law Forum. University of Maryland, Baltimore, Md.

Professional Geographer. Association of American Geographers, Washington, D.C.

Science. American Association for the Advancement of Science, Washington, D.C.

Technology Review. Massachusetts Institute of Technology, Cambridge, Mass.

University of Colorado Law Review. Knoss, Burton C. "Preparation of an Environmental Impact Statement." University of Colorado Law Review, Boulder, Colo., vol. 44, 1972.

U.S. Environmental Protection Agency, Environmental Impact Statement Guidelines, Washington, D.C.

PART 3

SYNTHESIS

INTRODUCTION

This final portion of the book illustrates several of the ways in which decision makers and planners can use the environmental assessment findings, including some of the more recent landscape planning procedures. For the most part, the procedures described are those that use the assessment techniques discussed in Part 2.

The specific landscape assessment presented in the preceding chapter as well as the composite environmental planning procedures discussed in this chapter may be used in making several general types of environmental planning decisions, each of which addresses different, although sometimes overlapping, requirements. These decisions have to do with preservation, protection, development, reclamation, and management. A brief definition of each follows.

Preservation decisions attempt to maintain a piece of land in its existing state. No direct human use is allowed, although indirect benefits to society may accrue from the preserved land. For example, it is often argued that coastal wetlands should be preserved in their natural state to maintain the uniform exchange of nutrients necessary to sustain marine food cycles, which in turn ensure the viability of fishing operations.

Protection, or conservation as it is also known, implies limited human use within specified guidelines. These guidelines are established to protect the most valued attributes of the protection area. A floodplain limited to agriculture use is a good example of a protection decision. The high-quality soils created by flood-borne sediments are protected from destruction by development; at the same time, no new residents will be exposed to the hazards of flooding.

Development decisions comprise the third category. As defined here, these decisions aim at transforming a rural landscape into an urban-metropolitan landscape. Structures are erected, and concentrated human interaction takes place in an area hitherto free from such activity. As used by planners, the term *development* includes all industrial, commercial, residential, transportation, and some intensive recreational uses.

Reclamation decisions have precisely the opposite intent of development decisions. The goal of reclamation decisions is to undo the damage caused by previous development or management decisions that in some way impaired an environmental resource. Corrective measures are applied in an attempt to reclaim that resource and to return it to its natural state or at least to improve upon its degraded state. The change of a riverfront from an industrial to a recreation use is an example of reclamation. Recreation uses are more compatible with the river and the shoreline landscape than are industrial uses. Reclamation of this kind has been done in many parts of Europe and the United States.

These first four types of decisions are what may be called "contextual" land use decisions. They decide which categories of land uses will go where. The fifth type of environmental decision—management strategies—specifies both the land use activities allowable and the strategies for managing these activities within each of the four land use decision areas. For example, a parcel set aside primarily as a groundwater recharge area may also be appropriate for low-density housing. In addition to determining land use directly, management restrictions may indirectly regulate the use of land. For example, in this same aquifer recharge area, there might be restrictions on the salting of icy roads during the winter in order to protect the groundwater quality of the area.

Environmental or landscape planning procedures are designed to synthesize available landscape assessments so that decision makers have the kind of environmental information necessary to make sensible land use and management decisions. In the following chapter, three procedures and their potential utility for decision making are discussed. None of the examples deals with all five types of environmental decisions. Instead, they have been selected to show how complex information can be abstracted and synthesized in meaningful form, for it is ultimately, of course, still the decision maker who has the final responsibility for determining trade-offs among alternative future landscape possibilities.

The three examples are not necessarily the best examples of landscape planning, but they do adequately represent the evolution of thinking in this field from the 1960s to the present. Because the author was involved in each of the studies described and, consequently, because he has a direct understanding of the problems and procedures related to each example, he can to some extent simplify the presentation of the procedures without the risk of distortion—which might be the result if he tried to interpret other researchers' intent on the basis of their final product.

It will be seen that during the past two decades, significant development has occurred in environmental planning. But planning is only as good as the findings that can be generated by the assessment techniques. The weaknesses and limitations of these techniques do not disappear in their synthesis; rather, they are frequently compounded. The apparent problems and limitations of current environmental planning, however, do not make the results of existing assessment techniques useless. They do indicate that these results must be used with caution and that research is still needed to improve environmental assessment and planning techniques so that their results may be increasingly relied upon.

9 LANDSCAPE PLANNING PROCEDURES

Much of the landscape planning of the 1960s was based on less detailed information than is now available with improved data-gathering and manipulation techniques. The procedures used during the 1960s have been characterized by Mabbutt, an Australian geographer, as the *landscape approach*. This approach usually consists of the compilation of several types of environmental resource data—concerning, for example, landform, soils, and vegetation. When this information is overlaid, areas with similar characteristics may be evaluated for planning decisions. For example, an area with steep hills, highly erodible soil types, and fragile vegetation might be identified as a discrete landscape type; knowing this, planners can have a limited notion of which land uses are appropriate for that type of area.

Although this degree of abstraction has obvious limitations, it has been very useful in planning. Key landscape attributes such as topography, soil, and vegetation are often sufficient for some kinds of large-scale decision making. They are also useful in areas where planning is to proceed in sequential stages. That is, by providing some general information about a large area, which can then be subject to a more detailed assessment and planning at a smaller scale, the landscape approach can provide the framework for later decisions.

More recently, with the aid of computers and geographic information systems (see Chapter 4), planners have gained the ability to describe many attributes of increasingly smaller land units in quantitative terms (as discussed in Part 2) and to combine them into composite values.

In addition to being more specific and quantitative, this *parametric approach* allows the values of various landscape attributes to be weighted differentially to account for their relative significance. These weightings are usually perceived economic, social, political, professional, or other values. Comparisons among the results of different weightings can also be readily made.

To provide a better understanding of the differences between the *landscape* and *parametric* approaches, each is discussed with two different examples. The parametric approach is shown using the planning model developed by the landscape research group at the University of Massachusetts, the group that developed several of the assessment procedures described in Part 2.

THE LANDSCAPE APPROACH

Before landscape planners used it, many geographers, geologists, and other scientists used a landscape approach to land classification.[1] Landscape planners began to adopt this approach in the 1950s. During the 1960s, however, it became much more widely used, in large part in response to the efforts of the Scottish-born landscape architect-planner, Ian McHarg.

McHarg and his firm applied the landscape approach to several metropolitan regional planning problems in the United States. They mapped various major landscape characteristics on individual maps and identified the values from highest to lowest of each landscape characteristic. They overlaid these values to see the composite pattern of high and low values from the point of view of conservation/preservation, recreation, and suitability for development. The final, composite map was then used as a basis for formulating sound landscape planning alternatives. *Design with*

Nature, the book in which McHarg eloquently described his environmental approach to land use planning, has had a significant impact on environmental planning both within and outside the planning field.[2]

During the 1960s, many other groups emerged in the United States and in Europe that applied similar landscape approaches to problems in environmental planning. Most of the environmental plans of this period were aimed at identifying those areas in which, from an environmental perspective, development either should not occur or should be limited. In other words, the great majority of these plans were oriented toward preservation and protection.

This emphasis can be seen in a study carried out on Nantucket Island in Massachusetts. In some later studies, the landscape approach was expanded to include an indication of where development should occur, given the characteristics of the land. The Boston metropolitan case study discussed below illustrates this added dimension.

The Nantucket Case Study. The beautiful, but fragile, island of Nantucket is located about thirty miles south of Cape Cod. During the 1960s it began to experience increasing growth pressures as many residents of the northeastern United States sought to enjoy its secluded amenities. Town officials became concerned about the rapid, unplanned growth generated by these "off-islanders." In 1966, with the help of the Massachusetts Department of Natural Resources, a team of scientific resource specialists (such as ecologists and wildlife biologists) and landscape planners was assembled to inventory and interpret the island's landscape resources. Resource inventories of varying degrees of specificity were mapped on individual inventory maps by the specialists. The landscape planners then grouped all the inventory maps into three categories using a landscape approach.[3]

Three categories of analysis were investigated. The first category combined and mapped eight wildlife and vegetative resources that were considered important by the scientists. For instance, certain coastal wetlands were important as rich breeding areas for shellfish. After combining the eight inventory maps, areas were mapped wherein at least three of the eight significant resources were found to exist. As a result, eight areas on the island were identified as important wildlife and vegetation resource areas deserving of either preservation or protection.

The second category of analysis included resource areas and hazard areas of such significance as to warrant preservation or protection. Among these were areas susceptible to periodic shoreline erosion and groundwater and recharge zones.

The third category identified landscapes with the highest visual quality and scenic view areas (see Figure 24). These areas were also recommended for protection from development.

The type of assessment map used in the Nantucket study may be used by decision makers in the same way as the individual assessment maps discussed in Part 2. The combination of the three maps, however, provided a more comprehensive basis for recommending environmental landscape preservation and protection. Figure 32 shows the synthesis of the three individual assessments discussed above. This final map illustrates the result of a relatively simple landscape planning approach aimed at controlling development. It is mainly a statement of where not to develop. It shows areas recommended for preservation or protection and for what reason. There are some areas in which two or three tones overlap: these areas were thought to require the most critical action. As a result of these recommendations, conservation groups on the island have, in the last decade, purchased several thousand acres of those lands recommended for preservation and protection.

The Boston Metropolitan Case Study for Guiding Growth. A more recent study using the landscape approach dealt with the so-called South Eastern New England (SENE) Region, which encompasses the metropolitan landscape stretching from Boston, Massachusetts, to Providence, Rhode Island. Supported by several federal and state agencies, the study was aimed at generating information that could aid in planning the future use of the region's water and

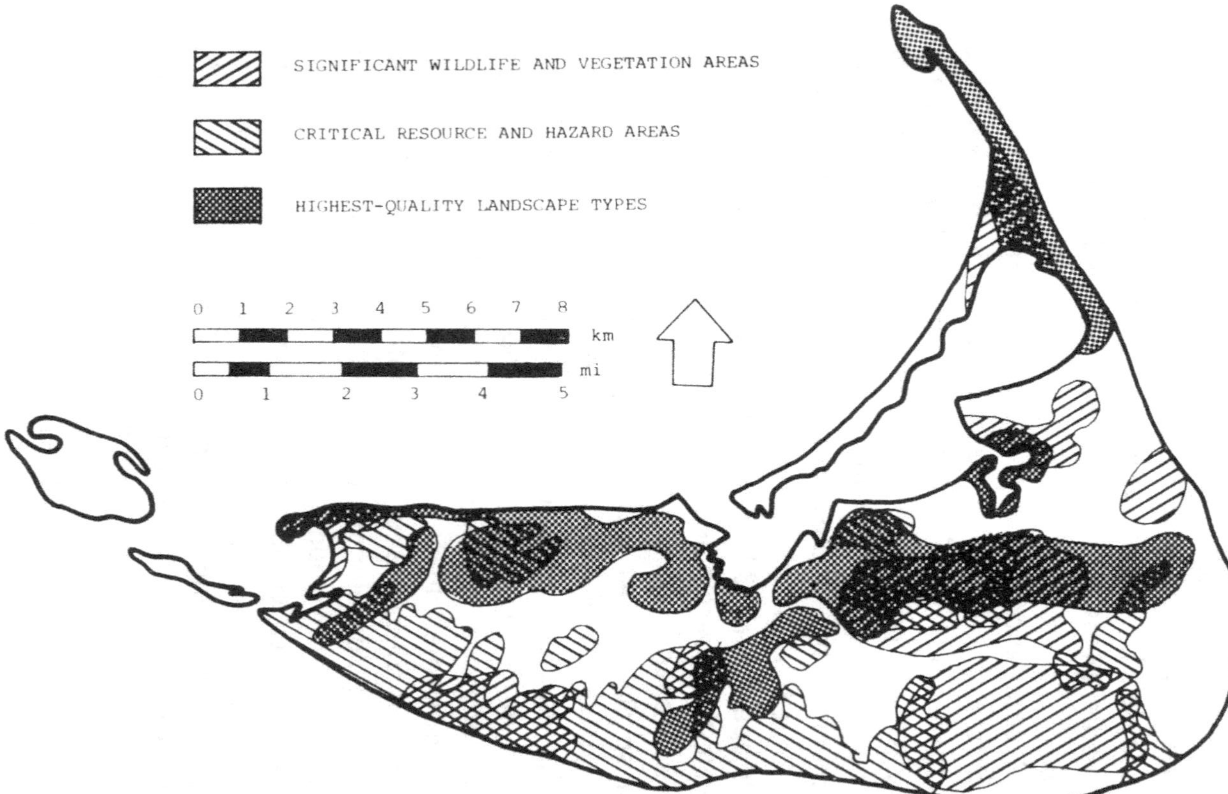

FIGURE 32. Landscape Synthesis, Nantucket, Massachusetts. The three separate resource and hazard assessment maps were combined to show the amount, distribution, and overlap of critical areas when using the landscape approach. This composite map was drawn by overlaying the three separate assessment maps prepared by the author in collaboration with Dr. Ervin Zube, study coordinator.

related land resources. In addition, the planners undertook to determine the region's capability for absorbing growth. By evaluating various environmental resource characteristics, the "resource holding capacity" of the region was estimated.[4] The results of this study dealing with the Boston region will be discussed in detail, thus permitting a comparison of these results with the earlier plans of Eliot (see Figure 12) and MacKaye (see Figure 13).

The SENE study addressed the same preservation and protection components as the Nantucket study. However, it also evaluated areas proposed for development. It assessed developmental suitability for all undeveloped areas for which preservation or protection was not recommended. It then proposed a future development density for the Boston region, a proposal based on the composite intrinsic characteristics of the various land units of this landscape. Figure 33 illustrates the three-phase process used to generate these recommendations. Each of the critical, highly valued resource and hazard areas was identified and assessed by a team of specialists that included hydrologists, soil scientists, geologists, wildlife biologists, foresters, recreation specialists, and others. The resource and hazard areas (after being grouped by the phases shown in Figure 33) were mapped by the landscape planners. Individual maps were then overlaid to produce composite assessment maps for each of these use categories: (1) preservation of critical resources, (2) protection of highly valued resources, and (3) development (at various densities) for all areas found suitable for development. The three composite assessment maps were further combined to produce a "Development Capabilities Map." This map is illustrative of an environmental landscape plan stemming from a generalized landscape approach, comparable to those of McHarg and others. An abstracted version of this map for the Boston region is shown in Figure 34.

The reader may wish to compare the SENE study (Figure 34) with the earlier work of Eliot (Figure 12) and MacKaye (Figure 13). These three illustrations, when compared, clearly show the evolution of environmental/landscape planning (see Chapter 3).

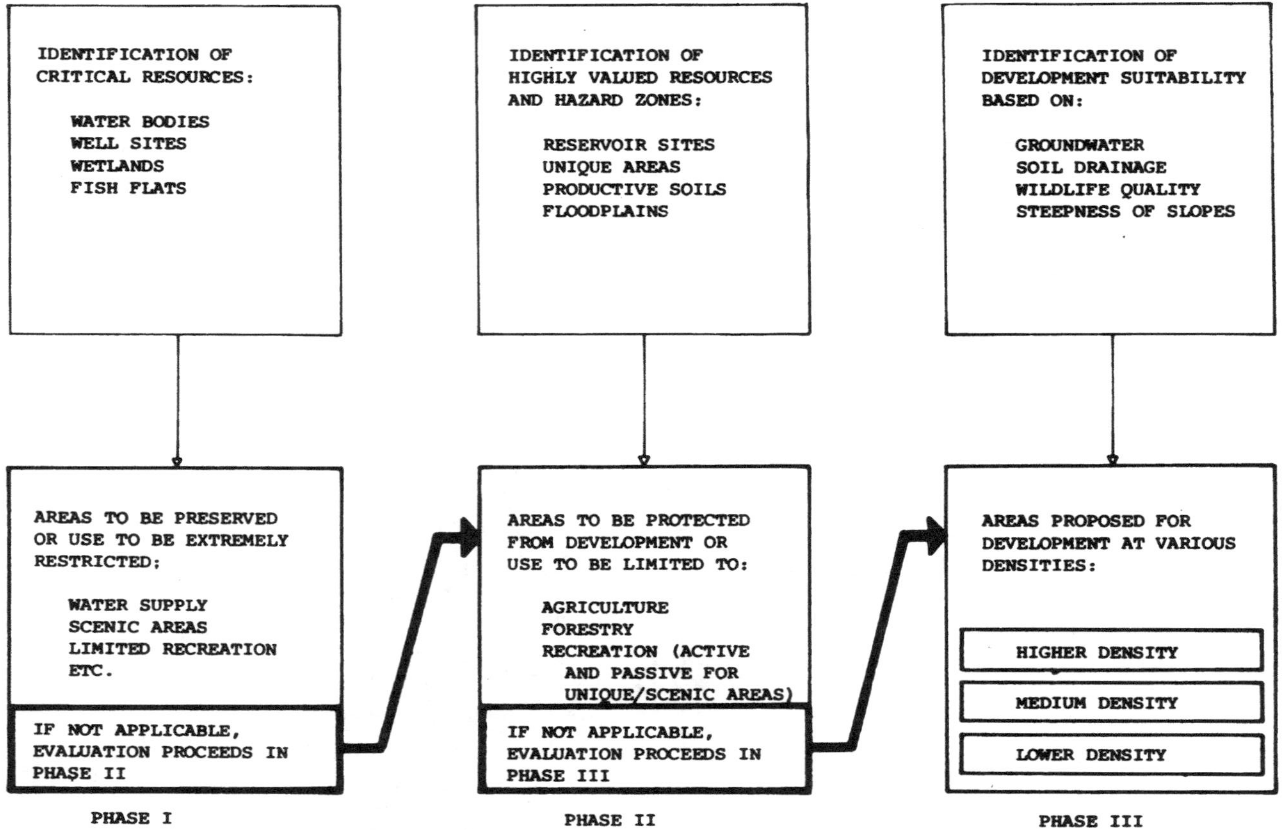

FIGURE 33. This simplified landscape approach attempts to deal with preservation, protection, and development types of environmental decisions. This planning process is abstracted from the work of T. J. Clapp and J. P. Wargo. The study was codirected by Dr. Ervin Zube and the author.

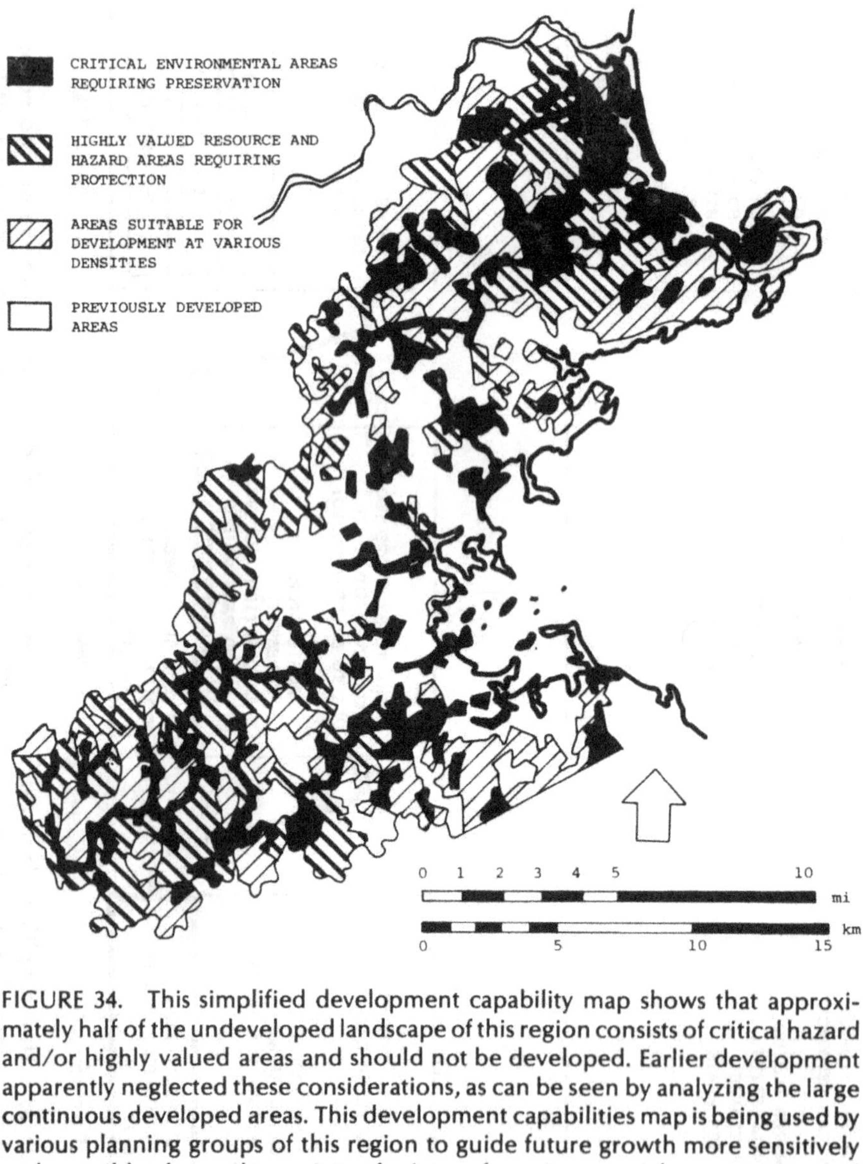

FIGURE 34. This simplified development capability map shows that approximately half of the undeveloped landscape of this region consists of critical hazard and/or highly valued areas and should not be developed. Earlier development apparently neglected these considerations, as can be seen by analyzing the large continuous developed areas. This development capabilities map is being used by various planning groups of this region to guide future growth more sensitively and sensibly from the point of view of environmental constraints and opportunities.

This latest of the three studies for the Boston region concludes that about half of the undeveloped landscape of this metropolitan region is characterized by resource values or hazardous characteristics of such significance that it should be recommended for preservation and protection from development.[5] This synthesis is useful for major decisions such as are involved in the location of a highway or the selection of a large tract of land for development. Results at this scale, however, are not useful for site-specific decisions. In contrast, the following discussion of the parametric approach can be used both for large-scale decisions of this type and for more specific decisions based on the composite values of much smaller portions of the landscape.

THE PARAMETRIC APPROACH

Advancements in the technology of remote sensing and computer graphics made the development of the parametric approach inevitable. Mabbutt summarizes the capabilities of the parametric approach as follows: "It achieves a more precise definition of land and . . . it avoids the subjectivity of a landscape method; being quantitative, it allows comparisons between and affords greater consistency within land evaluation projects; and it is in terms suited to automatic scanners and computers."[6]

Several of the more developed assessment techniques discussed in Part 2 exhibit parametric characteristics, including the assessment techniques for water quality, agriculture productivity, flood hazard, air pollution, and noise pollution. The adaptation of the parametric approach to the synthesis of several assessed values (i.e., to environmental planning), however, is still in its infancy, since the needed advancements in computer graphics (described in Chapter 4) have only recently been achieved.

A parametric approach in which large-sized grid cells are used has been available to planners since the late 1960s. However, because of the great loss in information detail due to the large size of the cells, the results of this approach were at this time not much better than those of the landscape approach. With the new, finer computerized grid systems now available, more acceptable specificity can be achieved, but it is still relatively expensive because it requires considerable computer time to run. Within a few years, however, more advanced and less expensive techniques will certainly be available for planners. As pointed out in Chapter 4, a more advanced computer graphic technique—the area boundary system—is already working in the laboratory. The landscape approach, though useful, may soon be a part of history.

Although computer programs are being developed for area boundary systems, experimentation with the computerized grid system for planning is going on in several research projects.[7] As an introduction to this developing environmental planning, let us describe some early results of the University of Massachusetts landscape research team. The individual assessment procedures described in Part 2, which were illustrated using some of the work of this group, are combined in this discussion in order to demonstrate the increased specificity and utility of the parametric approach for landscape planning.

The METLAND Landscape Planning Model. Figure 35 illustrates the conceptual framework of the parametric landscape planning process designed by the University of Massachusetts research team.[8] Its three phases of plannings tasks—assessment, evaluation, and implementation—have been specifically designed to address the environmental problems resulting from large-scale decentralization, although it is likely that the basic tripartite concept will have validity for other planning objectives as well.

The most research has been completed on the first, "assessment" phase of this model, as indicated by the greater detail shown for Phase I in Figure 35. This phase consists of four major components, which correspond to the four categories of environmental problems discussed in Chapter 2. Indeed, they include many of the assessment procedures for resources, hazards, development suitability, and ecological stability that have been presented in Part 2 of this book. The rest of this chapter will demonstrate how this preliminary parametric planning procedure tackles the problems of synthesizing the results of individual assessment findings, the problems of evaluating alternative planning options, and the consequences of potential land use "trade-off" decisions.

As discussed above, the landscape approaches of the 1960s often merely identified landscape values or hazard potentials, which, if significant, were handled as if each were of equal importance. This assumption, however, has often provided an inadequate basis for reconciling the competing economical, political, and social values that may operate in any given situation. One of the implicit advantages of a quantitative, parametric landscape assessment is that it is amenable to a variety of differential weightings to express a given value perspective. One of the weightings techniques explored in the Massachusetts research ascribes economic, dollar-per-acre values based on an analysis of the economic activities of the public with respect to the various landscape attributes. As shown in the evaluation phase in Figure 35, it is suggested that in environmental planning, several sets of values should be established. Sociopolitical and economic values should be expressed for both short-range and long-range goals. In the near future, the development of computerized quantitative techniques for illustrating the consequences of trade-offs among alternative sets of values will facilitate this task.

To illustrate how value differentiation can provide an input to environmental planning, varying values assigned to the landscape resources assessed for the town of Burlington, Massachusetts, are shown here in economic terms. The resource economists of the landscape research group derived value estimates relative to the Boston metropolitan region for the resource, hazard, and development suitability variables listed under Phase I in Figure 35.

The preparation of the composite resource value map for Burlington involves an overlay procedure similar to the one discussed in the landscape approach. As a first step, the maps shown in Figure 20 (high-yield and high-quality water resource areas), Figure 21 (high-quality and usable agricultural lands),

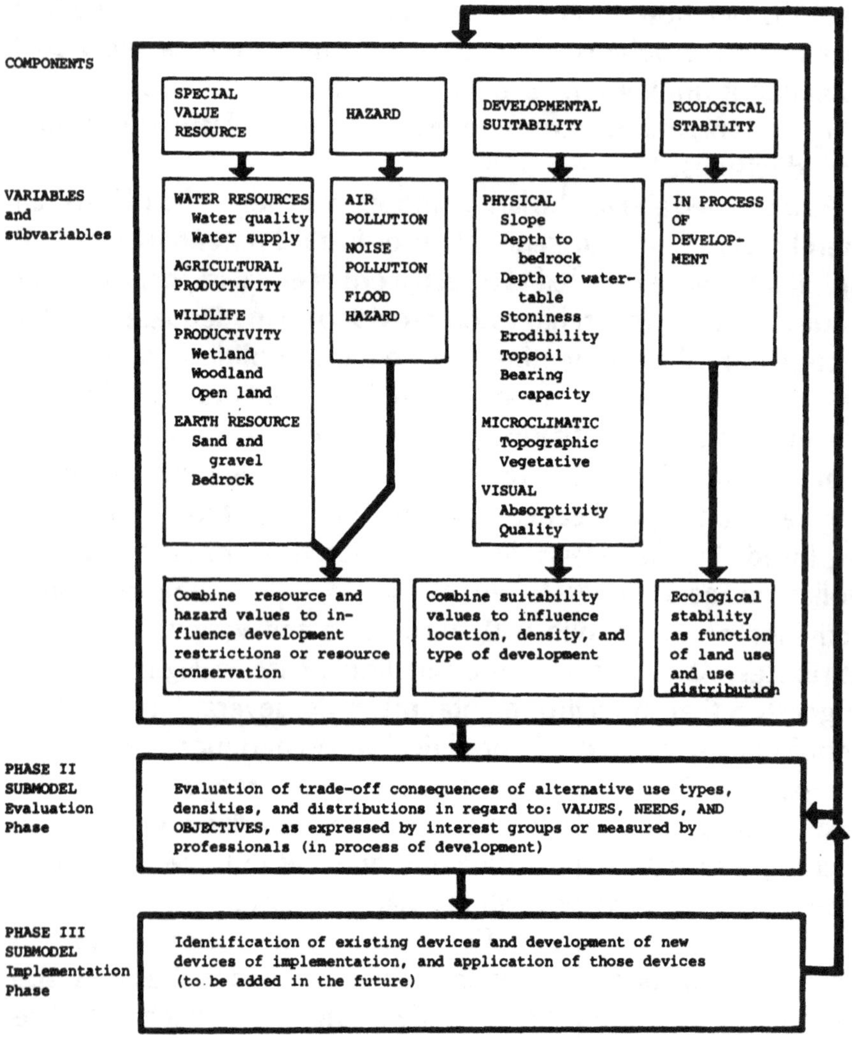

FIGURE 35. Conceptual framework of an environmental/landscape planning process. This figure represents the process developed and used by the University of Massachusetts landscape research group under the study acronym METLAND.

Figure 22 (high-quality wildlife habitat), and Figure 23 (areas with good sand and gravel potentials) are overlaid (Figure 36). The difference between this overlaying procedure and that used in the landscape planning approach, however, is twofold. First, the overlaying process is done more accurately by using a computer plotter. Second, each area shown on each individual assessment map may be assigned an estimated dollar value. The overlay thus shows not only where high-quality areas exist but also gives an indication of their relative significance resulting from the combined dollar values of the constituent resources. It should be noted, however, that owing to the small size of the map in Figure 36, only a range of low to high values is shown here. The computer, however, is capable of calculating both the estimated composite value per acre and the estimated composite value of each parcel of each combination.

The magnitude of the composite values of the special resources shown in Figure 36 is impressive. If these estimated values were to be confirmed, metropolitan growth, when implemented without regard to environmental values, would be shown to be very costly indeed. The reader is cautioned, however, not to take these value estimates as conclusive evidence of resource loss. However, this information does have two important uses. First, when probable areas of resource value concentration are known, growth can be directed away from these areas, assuming that sufficient alternative land is available. When and if, at a later date, these values are confirmed by detailed assessment techniques, such as drilling to find out actual depths and qualities of sand and gravel resources, more permanent management decisions may be made for the use of these areas. The second use of the information lies in the recognition that these overlapping values are not always additive. For example, excavation of sand and gravel in areas of high water supply potential may impair the rechargeability of groundwater or destroy certain wildlife habitat areas.

In addition to the assessment of the special critical resource values, the parametric approach can be used for assessing hazard-related value losses (e.g., from flood, air pollution, and noise pollution hazards) and development suitability values (including physical, microclimatic, and visual values). These hazard and suitability values have also been expressed in economic terms relative to the Boston metropolitan region.

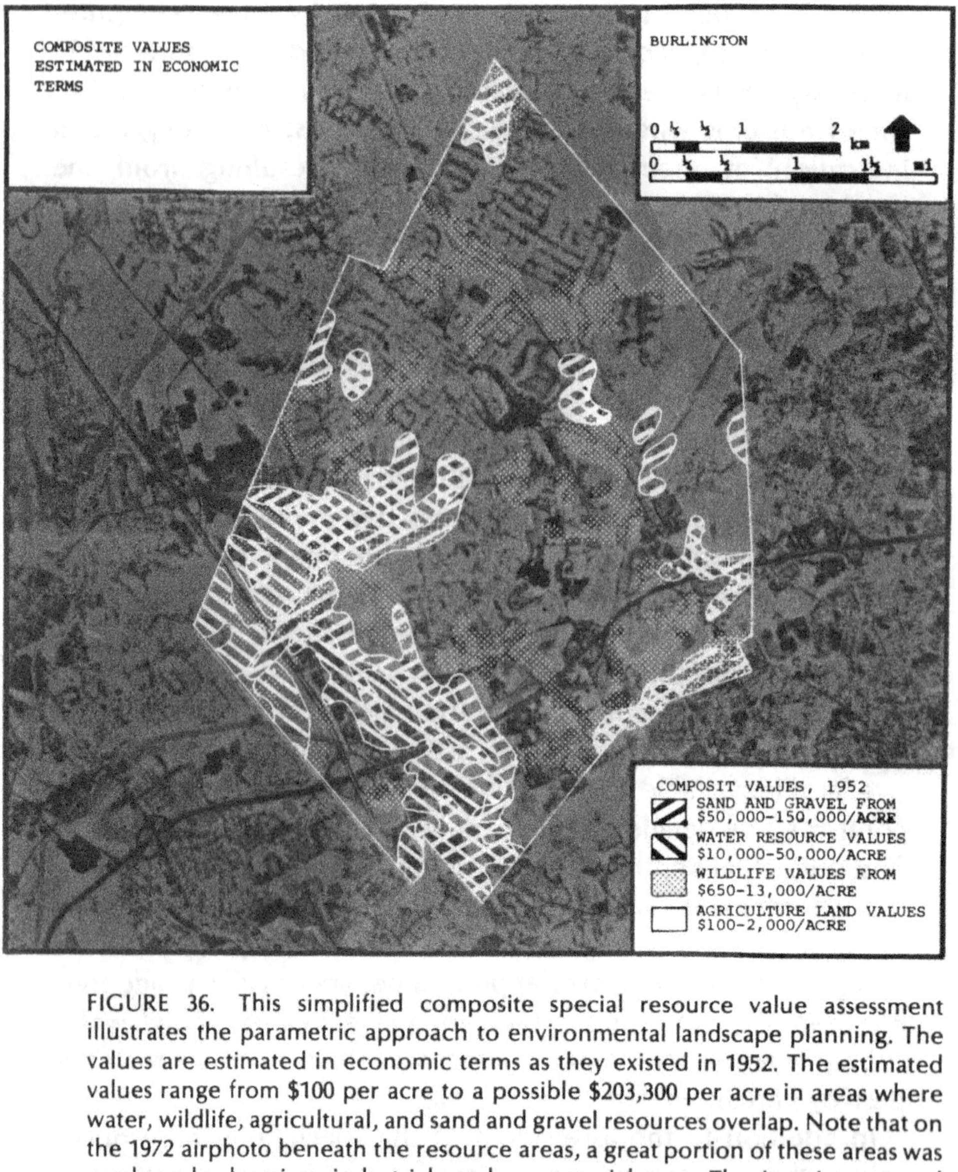

FIGURE 36. This simplified composite special resource value assessment illustrates the parametric approach to environmental landscape planning. The values are estimated in economic terms as they existed in 1952. The estimated values range from $100 per acre to a possible $203,300 per acre in areas where water, wildlife, agricultural, and sand and gravel resources overlap. Note that on the 1972 airphoto beneath the resource areas, a great portion of these areas was used up by housing, industrial, and commercial uses. The impairment and elimination of these resources is estimated at over $30 million.

This composite map was abstracted from the work of K. H. Ferris and S. J. Caswell, aided by J. Foster, R. Torla, and R. Whaley, resource economists, and by the author.

Finally, combined value estimates of resources, hazards, and development suitabilities have been prepared for 1952, before the major urbanization of Burlington, and again for 1971, by which time 75 percent of the town had been developed with low-density housing and commercial and industrial uses. Though the scale of the illustration does not permit a detailed breakdown of the changes in resource, hazard, and development suitability, Figure 37 does give an idea of what major abuses of resources occurred during the roughly twenty-year urbanization of the town of Burlington.

The conclusions presented here and shown in Figures 36 and 37 were guided by an economic attitude toward the environmental components considered. There are many other ways of weighting and manipulating the values of each environmental component and variable. For example, conservation groups, town officials, recreation specialists, and developers might ascribe values to these landscape characteristics differently. The actions they desire might also have very dissimilar consequences. The possibility of conducting this multifaceted type of planning and synthesis, however, is now within our reach. Once value judgment survey procedures yield sufficiently reliable results, these results can then be easily weighted, manipulated, and simulated to show the consequences of alternative planning strategies.

This author advocates an evaluation and planning process such as the one described above. This multifaceted process is proposed for the following reasons. First, since all planning is a learning process, the environmental planner should not represent the views of a single person. In the same way, environmental decisions should be influenced by many, nonexperts as well as experts. Second, since the information upon which we base these environmental decisions is also changing, we should be sensitive to this dynamic process. For instance, sound ecological input is not yet available for planning purposes (see Chapter 8). But this input will probably be available in the near future and promises to be of great importance to planning and decision making.[9]

Environmental planners and decision makers, therefore, should

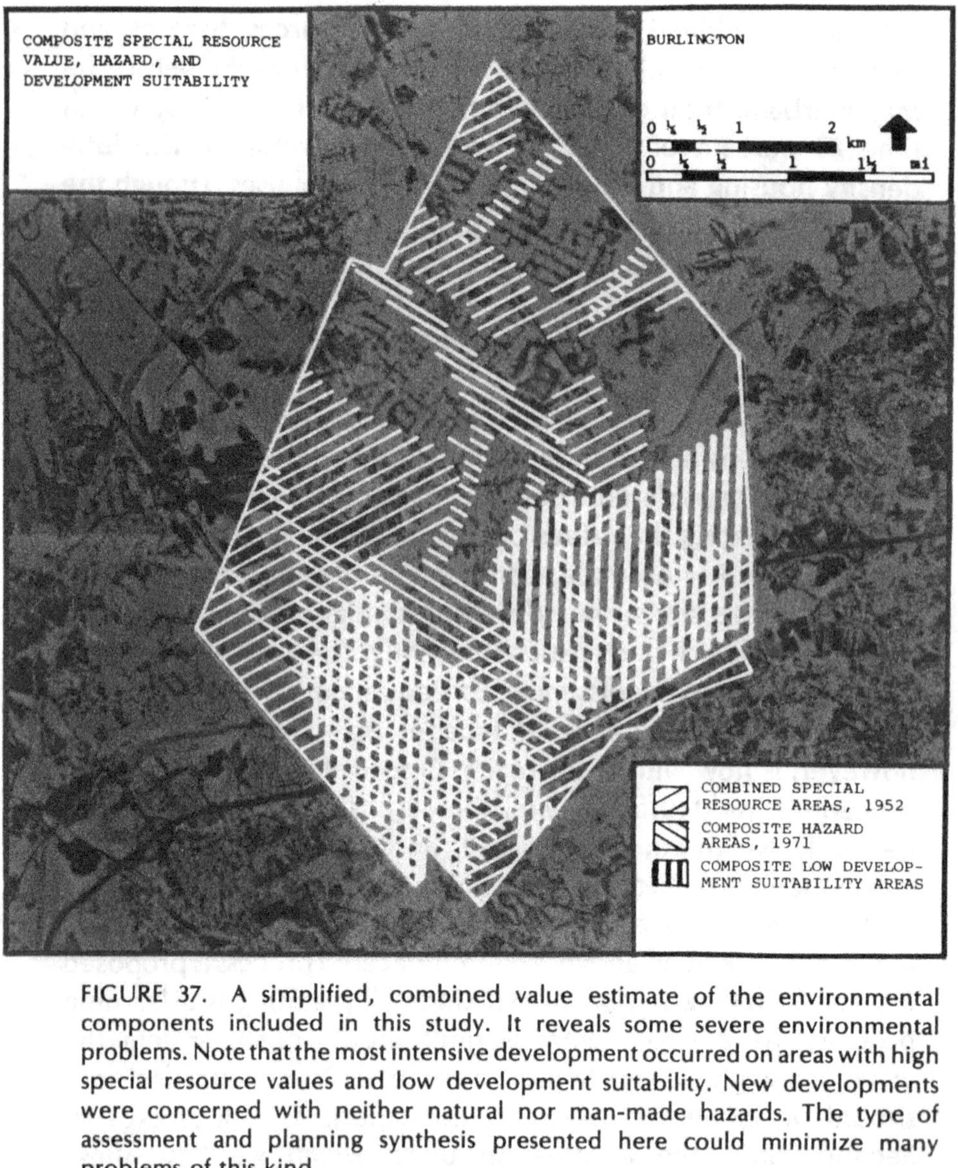

FIGURE 37. A simplified, combined value estimate of the environmental components included in this study. It reveals some severe environmental problems. Note that the most intensive development occurred on areas with high special resource values and low development suitability. New developments were concerned with neither natural nor man-made hazards. The type of assessment and planning synthesis presented here could minimize many problems of this kind.

This map is based on the work of K. H. Ferris, a landscape planner of the University of Massachusetts landscape research group.

not make definitive plans. Instead, they should strive to make the best possible proposal and decision at any one time based on all the available information. They should base their plans on the widest possible inputs of the population and the pertinent disciplines while allowing for future modifications. With open minds and proper use of the assessment and planning techniques discussed in this book, we could significantly improve the metropolitan and megalopolitan environments in which most of us live. In itself, of course, this method is not an answer to potential global environmental problems. Nevertheless, if our concern in dealing with decentralization is recognized, we will undoubtedly enhance our understanding of the relationship of human beings to the environment—which is necessary to improving that relationship at any scale.

NOTES

1. J. A. Mabbutt, "Review of Concepts of Land Classifications," in *Land Evaluation,* ed. G. A. Stewart (Melbourne, Australia: Macmillan Co., 1968) pp. 15-21.
2. I. L. McHarg, *Design with Nature* (Garden City, N.Y.: The Natural History Press, 1969).
3. E. H. Zube and C. A. Carlozzi, eds., *An Inventory and Interpretation: Selected Resources of the Island of Nantucket,* Publication no. 4, Cooperative Extension Service, University of Massachusetts, Amherst, Mass., 1967.
4. J. T. Clapp and J. P. Wargo, *A Resource Holding Capacity Model for the Southeastern New England Study,* A Terminal Project, Department of Landscape Architecture, University of Massachusetts, Amherst, Mass., June 1974.
5. R. F. Gregg, R. D. Brown, and R. Kasvinsky, *How to Guide Growth in Southeastern New England* (Boston, Mass.: New England River Basin Commission, 1975).
6. Mabbutt, "Review of Concepts," pp. 21-22.
7. J. Gy. Fabos and K. H. Ferris, "The Utility of Second Generation Computer Graphic Tools in Environmental/Landscape Planning," in *Proceedings of World Organization of General Systems and Cybernetics:*

The Third International Congress in Bucharest, Romania, at Blackburn College of Technology, Blackburn, England, World Organization of General Systems and Cybernetics, forthcoming.

8. J. Gy. Fabos and S. J. Caswell, *Composite Landscape Assessment: Assessment Procedures for Special Resources, Hazard, and Development Suitability; Part II of the Metropolitan Landscape Planning Model (METLAND)*, Research Bulletin no. 637, University of Massachusetts, Agricultural Experiment Station, Amherst, Mass., January 1977.

9. J. Gy. Fabos, C. Greene, and S. A. Joyner, *The METLAND Landscape Planning Process: Composite Landscape Assessment, Alternative Plan Formulation and Plan Evaluation*, University of Massachusetts, Agricultural Experiment Station, Amherst, Mass., forthcoming.

SUGGESTED READINGS

Books

Hackett, B. *Landscape Planning*. Newcastle-on-Tyne, England: Oriel Press, 1971.

MacKaye, B. *The New Exploration: A Philosophy of Regional Planning*. Urbana: University of Illinois Press, 1962.

McHarg, I. L. *Design with Nature*. Garden City, N.Y.: Natural History Press, 1969.

Marsh, P. *Man and Nature*. Cambridge, Mass.: The Belknap Press of Harvard University Press, 1965.

Powell, J. W. *Report on the Lands of the Arid Regions of the United States*. Cambridge, Mass.: Belknap Press of Harvard University, 1962.

Stewart, A., ed. *Land Evaluation*. South Melbourne: Macmillan of Australia, 1968.

Zube, E.; Brush, R.; and Fabos, J. Gy., eds. *Landscape Assessment: Values, Perceptions and Resources*. Pt. 3. Stroudsburg, Pa.: Dowden, Hutchinson, and Ross, 1975.

Periodicals

Ekistics. Athens Center for Ekistics, Athens, Greece.

International Journal of Environmental Studies. Gordon and Breach Science Publishers, London.

Landscape. Berkeley, Calif.
Landscape Architecture. American Society of Landscape Architects, McLean, Va.
Landscape Planning. Elsevier Scientific Publishing Co., Amsterdam.

INDEX

www.ingramcontent.com/pod-product-compliance
Lightning Source LLC
LaVergne TN
LVHW011132300926
849160LV00008B/613
9780367298463